T0110283

WELLNESS IN INDIAN
FESTIVALS & RITUALS

WELLNESS IN INDIAN FESTIVALS & RITUALS

Since the Supreme Divine is
manifested in all the Gods, worship
of any God is quite legitimate.

J MOHAPATRA

B.E.(EL), BOE, PGDEEM
Formerly Executive Director, NTPC Ltd

PARTRIDGE
A Penguin Random House Company

Copyright © 2013 by J Mohapatra.

ISBN: Hardcover   978-1-4828-1691-4
             Softcover   978-1-4828-1690-7
             Ebook   978-1-4828-1689-1

All rights reserved. No part of this book may be used or reproduced by any means, graphic, electronic, or mechanical, including photocopying, recording, taping or by any information storage retrieval system without the written permission of the publisher except in the case of brief quotations embodied in critical articles and reviews.

Because of the dynamic nature of the Internet, any web addresses or links contained in this book may have changed since publication and may no longer be valid. The views expressed in this work are solely those of the author and do not necessarily reflect the views of the publisher, and the publisher hereby disclaims any responsibility for them.

To order additional copies of this book, contact
Partridge India
000 800 10062 62
www.partridgepublishing.com/india
orders.india@partridgepublishing.com

CONTENTS

WELLNESS BY OUR BELIEFS & CUSTOMS

WELLNESS BY OUR WORSHIPS, FESTIVALS & RITES

DEDICATION

This book is dedicated to my esteemed parents,
who were great believers of religious rites & customs and
used to celebrate all festivals prevailing in our society
with keen faith and trust for the well being of
thier children, family and the community.

J. Mohapatra

FOREWORD

Beyond The Rituals

Indian customs and rituals not only add value to life but also they are essential tools to connect to the Self. These rituals and customs have their foundation on scientific spirituality. Use of scientific knowledge for solving problems in our life and use of spiritual knowledge for attaining 'Moksha' (Liberation) through positive philosophy has been advised in our scriptures.

Rituals have been ordained to fulfil man's desires to help him live in harmony with his physical environment, to pay homage to his departed ancestors, to appease the Gods and finally to aid his spiritual ascent. Following such a way of life has helped man to maintain equilibrium between his body, mind and soul as well as with his family and society.

Social cohesion of man is important for leading a fulfilled life. One of the key factors that contribute towards strengthening social cohesion is rituals. These bring individuals together for a mutually beneficial purpose. Man being a social animal needs people to survive and to lead a healthy life.

In today's increasingly organized, technological, intellectual and materialistic world, there is a correspondingly increasing trend to consider these rituals old—fashioned, unscientific and unnecessary. But the reality is that these rituals have been simplified by our ancient scientists, the 'Great Gurus' (Preceptors) so as to help the common man to inculcate such values into their daily life. This is how since a long time, Indians who have understood the true value and scientific basis of such rituals have been leading a much disciplined life.

It is every person's right to follow the age-old rituals based on their merits available and from the self experience. It is our right and duty to understand scientifically, rationally and logically the meaning of each and every ritual and to follow the same in our life systematically.

Aachaarath labhathe hi ayu:
Aachaarath dhanamakshayam
Aachaarath labhathe suprajaa:
Aachaaro ahanthya lakshanam

Rituals or 'achaaranas' are followed for the psychological and physiological health and long life, they are followed for prosperity and wealth; They are followed for strong family and social cohesion and following such rituals give a fine personality, positive outlook and vision.

This book has been written to impart knowledge about Indian customs and rituals in a simple and lucid way. Such knowledge of life messages will reach every home through this book and the present generation will reap its benefits immensely.

Ratna Samanta
Faculty, Delhi Public School

PREFACE

The events, rituals and customs projected in this book are facts which are followed in Indian society as popular practice and traditional beliefs. Most of them are celebrated as variety of customs in different parts of India although some have been lost. There are interesting incidents with spiritual observations of God-Worshiping and group prayers which continue with keen faith and trust from generation to generation.

All these rituals are aimed to secure the welfare and developments in life. The Supreme, all-power-God manifests on earth as different incarnations. By the law of action (karma), the soul reaps fruits, good or bad according to past and present activities. It is believed that the moral soul is continuously born and reborn in numerous species until it attains liberation. Rightousness, religion, duty, responsibility, virtue, justice, goodness and truth are treated as Divine law. It is a way of life and is called as Eternal Religion.

India is a land of great tolerance and every Indian is allowed to worship any religion in a church, mosque or gurudwara as freely as he does in a temple. It offers great freedom of worship and insists that each person must be guided by his or her own individual spiritual experience. It is said that, if there is one place on face of the earth where all the dreams of living men have found a home from the very earliest age when man began the dream of existence, it is India.

In Indian philosophy it is believed that every act or deed must necessarily be followed by its consequences, which are not merely of a physical character, but also mental and moral. The inequalities in all walks of life between men in worldly position, their happiness and suffering are due to their actions in either the present or past life. In this life, the pleasure and misery experienced by a person is due to his deeds in the present or previous birth. Action (Karma) is originally a sort of account of debits and credits, a reckoning to be settled at the end of a life; actions may not create, but can adjust the effects of good or bad deeds.

The purpose of every person should be to get relieved of the bondage of rebirths and to achieve moksha / liberation from existence. There exists one Supreme Divine Being, eternal and unknowable which is manifested in all the Gods and all religions of men. He is spiritual, real, and omnipresent and exists in nature as well as inside the man. Since He is manifested in all the Gods, the worship of any God is quite legitimate.

This book depicts the experience of Indian rites, manners, customs, festivals and religious activities with ardent faith upon God which purifies wordly activities to lead sacred moral life.

J. Mohapatra

B-2/504, Krishna Apra Gardens,
Indirapuram, Distt. Ghaziabad,
U.P. - 201 014.
Ph.   :   011-26143111 (Off)
            0120-4564113 (Res.)
Mob. :   9717212999
E-mail :   mohapatraj6@gmail.com

Phase I

1. **Mystical Indian Customs**

   (a) Lady's Hair Parting & applying vermillion, (b) Hygienically carrying a child, (c) Child's Intellectual well being,(d) Longevity Ceremony, (e) Worshipping Goddess Shasthi (f) New-born's name giving, (g) Child's first outing, (h) Child's first feeding, (i) Mother's protégé, (j) Tonsure ceremony, (k) Ear piercing ceremony,(l) Protective horse shoe, (m) Learning of alphabets.

2. **Ensuring Goodluck**

   There is popular belief of wearing amulet, bracelet, necklace, ring, talisman etc prepared out of God-worshipping and sacred chanting to acquire spiritual power for good health.

3. **Ayurvedic Practitioner**

   In rural India treatment of illnesses are invariably taken by villagers from Kabiraj / Vaidya who cures patients by ayurvedic methods.

4. **Commencement Ceremony**

   A child undergoes the rituals for beginning of learning at the tender age before he is admitted to any formal schooling.

5. **Initiation (Upanayana / Janeo)**

   It is performed before marriage and is popularly known as thread ceremony by which a child is initiated into the vow of Guru, the Vedas, the Restraints, Observances and the vicinity of a God, thus preparing the youth to lead a systematic and more responsible life onwards.

6. **Veneration to Lord Satyanarayan**

   Parents perform worshipping of Lord Naryan by the priest at their house every year on the child's birthday for his well being.

7. **Kid's Gratification (Bal Leela)**

   Some affluent parents on every birthday of their child arrange for cooking and mass feeding to local kids in village temple premises to obtain children's blessings for the well being of the child.

8. **Chorus of Rhythmic Chants (Ashtaprahari)**

   This is a nonstop rhythmic mass chanting of Lord Krishna continuing for 8 Prahars (32 hrs). This is spiritual celebration of continuously uttering God's name by groups of devotees without stop.

9. **Deity's Holy Bath, Archana and Vision**

   People with deep devotion, desire to have the morning glimpse of their reputed local God and Goddess by offering morning bath to the Deity with holy water sandal paste, oil, vermillion, new clothing, garlands and doing 'Archana' by burning ghee lamps.

10. **Social Invocation to Lord Shiva**

    Worship of Lord Shiva takes place in local community-place or at village cross roads by group of neighbouring houses organizing a small spiritual fair with desire of prevailing goodness in the society.

11. **Adored Preceptor (Guru)**

    Number of preceptors (Guru) are adored by Indian people accepting as their mentor. They are popular among certain groups of people in the society who ardently follow their principles and worships him / her as God-Man / Woman.

12. **Pilgrimage to a notable shrine**

    There are several reputed shrines in India as per popular belief, visiting these shrines for a holy vision (Darshan) brings salvation to life.

13. Holy dip in sacred river

The most significant Hindu spiritual gathering in India is performed at pilgrims—centres such as Allahbad, Haridwar, Ujjain, Nashik, Chandrabhaga etc. Thousands of pilgrims take bath there during 'Kumbh Mela' with the desire of liberation (Moksha / Nirvana)

14. Hindu marriage ceremony

Hindu marriage is one of the major sacraments of life. It is a union of bride and groom and also their families. Customs of marriage differ from region to region, village to village but hymns chanted in Sanskrit are almost same in all parts of India. The rituals and methods of marriage ceremony are projected in detail.

WELLNESS BY OUR WORSHIPS, FESTIVALS & RITES

1.	Invocation to Sun God (Shamba Dashmi)	January
2.	Makar Sankranti (Pongal)	January
3.	Bonfire (Agni Utsav)	Jan-Feb
4.	Basant Panchami (Saraswati Puja)	February
5.	Maha Shivratri	March
6.	Festival of Colours (Holi)	Mid March
7.	Navratra & Ram Navami	March
8.	Easter & Good Friday	April
9.	First Baisakh (Baisakhi)	Mid April
10.	Bihu Festival	Mid April
11.	Mahavir Jayanti	April
12.	Devotional HorseDance	Apr / May
13.	Imperishable Day (Akshaya Tritiya)	Apr / May
14.	Budha Purnima	May
15.	Immaculate Observance (Sabitri)	June
16.	Divine Wedding (Shital Sasthi)	May / June
17.	Festive Earth (Raja Festival)	June
18.	Car Festival (Rath Yatra)	June-July
19.	Teej Festival	July / Aug
20.	Rain swept New Moon (Chitau Amabasya)	July

21.	Sacred Thread of Love (Raksha Bandhan)	August
22.	Id Ul Fitr	August
23.	Virgin's Solemnity	Aug-Sept
24.	Birth of Divinity (Janmashtami)	August
25.	Onam	September
26.	God of the Masses (Sri Ganesh)	September
27.	Divine Craftsman (Vishwakarma)	September
28.	Partaking New Grain (Nabanna)	September
29.	Mahalaya Obsequies (Shraddh)	September
30.	Dussehera	October
31.	Youthful Moon (Kumar Purnima)	October
32.	Festival of Lights (Diwali)	October
33.	Karva Chauth	October/November
34.	Sacrosanct Moon (Kartik Purnima)	November
35.	Prathma Ashtami	November
36.	Chhat Puja	November
37.	Muharram	November
38.	Glory of Goddess Mahalaxmi	Nov-Dec
39.	Blooming New Moon (Bakul Amabasya)	December
40.	Christmas	December

PHASE II

India is a land full of festivals with diverse cultures and religions. In these festivals, people celebrate joys of life with rituals, songs, hymns, dances, fasts and fists. Some festivals have occurred on fixed dates and most of the festivals are according to the calendars followed by different religions. Such important 40 festivals and fairs are described in 40 chapters

1. **Invocation to Sun-God (Shamba Dashmi)**
   This festival is celebrated in January at Eastern part of India. People worship the Sun-God for the well being of their family. Ladies keep fasting and worship the Sun-God in their open courtyard looking the Sun in the sky three times a day at sunrise, noon and sunset.

2. **Makar Sankranti (Pongal)**
   This festival is celebrated throughout the country known as Makar Sankranti and as Pongal in South India. People perform special worships with Makar grain and Revdi sweets as Prasad and offer to Gods. People give charity to the poor; friends and colleagues establish bosom relationship. It is a harvest festival in Southern India, especially in Tamil Nadu.

3. **Bon Fire (Agni Utsav)**
   It is a seasonal harvest festival called as Lohri in Delhi, Punjab, Haryana and Agni Utsav in Eastern India. Foot tapping, Bhangra Dance, Giddha Dance takes place. Fire God is worshipped with offering of Revdi, Sweets, Popcorn, Peanut, sesame, Parched rice and Sugarcane.

4. Basant Panchami (Saraswati Puja)

Goddess Saraswati who bestows the gift of education, music, dance and the arts is worshiped on this day.

5. Maha Shivratri

Worship of Lord Shiva continues all through the day and night. Devotees observe strict fast in honour of Lord Shiva. Women pray for the well being of their husband, unmarried women pray for an ideal husband.

6. Festival of Colours (Holi)

People of all cast, colour and creed forget their differences, old amnesties; assemble in their community-places, clubs, roads, markets, courtyards and houses to sprinkle on them the colour called 'Gulal', 'Abeer', smear all sorts of colours, spray coloured waters on everybody, embrace each other and exchange best wishes.

7. Nav Ratra & Ram Navami

It is a festival prevalent in north India and is known as Chaitra Navratri or Spring Navratri or Vasant Navratri or Ram Navratri and is dedicated to the worship of the Hindu Godess Durga, Lakshmi and Saraswati. The ninth day known as Ramnavami is the birthday celebration of Lord Rama.

8. Easter & Good Friday

Good Friday is the day on which Jesus was crucified and **Easter** day is the day on which Jesus came back to life. On **Easter Sunday** Christians believe Jesus Christ was resurrected from the dead and God's kingdom of love and forgiveness was established. Therefore, Christians exchange good wishes amongst themselves on this day.

9. First Baisakh (Baisakhi)

First day of the month of Baisakh is called 'Bishuba Sankranti' or 'Baishakhi'. Tradition of offering water, buttermilk, soft drinks, cold water to the thirsty at road side and at different places to mitigate sufferings from the scorching summer heat. People perform ceremonial functions, God worships and oblation.

10. Bihu Festival

This is the celebration of sowing season and is the most popular festival of Assam. At several places, Bihu fairs are organised where people participate in the games and other fun filled activities.

11. Mahavir Jayanti

The most important Jain festival, **Mahavir Jayanti** is celebrated on the thirteenth day of the Chaitra month of rising moon to commemorate the birthday of Lord Mahavir who was a saint and founder of **Jain** religion. It is a peaceful religion that cherishes simplicity.

12. Devotional Horse Dance

In east cost of India, this is about worship of the horse-faced Goddess 'Baseli', the tutelary goddess of the dynasty of fishermen who perform the famous folk dance known as horse-dance.

13. Imperishable Day (Akshaya Tritiya)

This is an auspicious day in the month of May i.e. third day of lunar Baisakh. Whatever noble work done on this day yields good result and remains forever as imperishable. The various activities like sowing seed, marriage, thread ceremony, constructions, inaugurations, may-fair etc are performed.

14. Buddha Purnima

Gautam Buddha was born on this day in 526 B.C. and attained **Nirvana** or enlightenment on this day. Buddha found his moksha and died on this very day. To commemorate Lord Buddha's three major events, birth, enlightenment and demise; this day is celebrated.

15. Immaculate Observance (Sabitri)

It occurs normally beginning of June every year. Married ladies, celebrate this immaculate religious observance for the good health, long life and good fortune of their husbands.

16. Divine Wedding (Shital Sasthi)

Shital Sasthi means indication of beginning of coolness after scorching heat of the month of May is observed in first week of June every year. This is a great festival of Lord Shiva whose marriage ceremony is performed with Goddess Parvati.

17. Festive Earth (Raja Festival)

'Raja' is a popular festival relating to earth which is compared to a lady. The earth becomes menstruated in this period and is ready for sowing of paddy seeds. In the month of 'Ashadh', in mid June every year, the famous Raja festival appears. It is celebrated in coastal districts of Odisha for 3 consecutive days in a grand manner by all sections of people specially the virgin girls.

18. Car Festival (Rath Yatra)

Lord Jagannath's car festival (Rath Yatra) takes place in the month of Ashadh (July). Three giant chariots each carrying the Gods, Jagannath, Balbadhra, Subhadra are pulled by devotees on the grand road of Puri town among millions of devotees.

19. Teej Festival

It is celebrated in North India heralding the onset of the monsoon season after the oppressive summer season. It is the festival of women folk commemorating Goddess Parvati's union with Lord Shiva and is celebrated for marital bliss, well being of spouse, children and purification of body and soul.

20. Rain Swept New Moon (Chitau Amabasya)

The rainy new moon day of Shravan at the end of July is an agricultural festival in eastern part of India, where farmers worship the paddy fields. On this occasion a special cake is prepared and offered to God and to the corn field and aquatic animals.

21. Sacred Thread of Love (Raksha Bandhan)

Full moon day of Shravan in middle of August is called 'Rakshi Purnima' or 'Raksha Bandhan'. It is the festival about affection, fraternity and sublime sentiments in India and specially is bond protection by a brother to his sister who ties, the sacred thread of love, 'Rakshi' on his wrist.

22. Id-Ul-Fitr

Eid-Ul-Fitr popularly known as Eid is the most auspicious festival observed by the muslim community to celebrate the conclusion of the month of fasting, Ramzan (Ramadan) and symbolizes a reward for their fasting. The significance of this festival is interpreted as a good time to bring people together in harmony and gratitude.

23. Virgin's Solemnity (Khuda Rukuni)

In the coastal districts of Eastern India, it is celebrated by the virgins on all five Sundays of Bhadrav (August-September). Goddess Durga is the presiding Deity and she likes the baked-broken-rice called 'Khuda'.

24. Birth of Divinity (Janmashtami)

It happens in the month of August every year and is significant as birthday of Lord Krishna who had manifested Himself as an incarnation to destroy the wicked, the unrighteousness and to establish virtue in earth.

25. Onam

It is celebrated in the state of Kerala every year in early September to rejoice the home coming of the famous benevolent king Mahabali to his own state. It is celebrated by people of all religion and communities.

26. God of the Masses (Shri Ganesh)

It is called Vinayak Chaturthi or Ganesh Puja and is celebrated by worshipping of Lord Ganapati (leader of masses), the queller of all obstacles (Vighneshwar) with great fervour in the state of Maharashtra, Gujarat, Andhra Pradesh, Odisha and in some part of other Indian states.

27. Divine Craftsman (Vishwakarma)

As popular Hindu belief, Lord Vishwakarma is the presiding deity of industries, crafts, architecture and engineering. He is worshipped throughout the country in all industrial places, machineries, factories, workshops, manufacturing plants and production units.

28. Partaking New Grain (Nabanna)

This festival is celebrated in East-Chhattisgarh and West Odisha on 5th day of bright fortnight of Bhadrav (September). It is believed that on this day, offering of the first harvest of the year to the God brings happiness in life, crops grow abundantly and the house gets enriched with wealth.

29. Mahalaya Obsequies (Shraddh)

The new moon day of Ashwin (September) is called 'Mahalaya'. On this day, Hindus offer obsequies (Shraddh) in honour of their ancestors by memorizing and expressing their obligations to them.

30. Dussehra (Vijay Dashmi)

Durga Puja in eastern India and in city of Mysore is famous, as worshipping the Goddess wipes out Durgati i.e. troubles. She is worshipped with great grandeur during Dussehra in the month of October.

31. Youthful Moon (Kumar Purnima)

The full moon night of month Ashwin (October) is called 'Kumar Purnima' which is a tradition of worship by young boys and girls (Kumar and Kumari) of Goddess Lakshmi.

32. Festival of Lights (Diwali)

Diwali is celebrated on new moon day of month of Kartik (Oct/ Nov). Everybody decorates his house by lighting lamps, candles, illuminating various types of coloured electric lights and worship the Goddess. Diwali evening is enjoyable with variety of lights and bursting of crackers.

33. Karva Chauth

'Karva Chauth' festival is celebrated in north and north-western part of India. It falls in the month of Karthik (Oct / Nov). A fast is kept by the married women to secure the long life of her husband. Women sit in circle with Puja thali collectively singing and performing the 'Fery'.

34. Sacrosanct Moon (Karthik Purnima)

Full moon day of month of Karthik (Nov) is called 'Karthik Poornima' or Ras Poornima'. People visit temple pray god, join mass eulogy, read epics, religious books and serve to the poor.

35. Prathma Ashtami

The 8th day of dark fortnight of month of 'Margashir' is called 'Prathma Ashtami'. Prathma Ashtami is a rite held for the life and prosperity of eldest child who is offered new clothes, smeared with vermillion, sandal paste, flowers and lighted lamp ovation by the mother and senior female relatives followed by elaborate rituals.

36. Chhat Puja
In eastern India, especially in the state of Bihar, East U.P and Jharkhand, 'Chaat Puja' is an important festival. This festival occurs twice in a year during month of Baisakh (May) and Kartik (November). The community festival is celebrated in honour of the Sun God.

37. Muharram
Muharram festival commemorates the martyrdom of **Hazrat Imam Hussain's**, violent death. This day awakens the sympathy of the faithful with sorrow and indignation. People observe Muharram for 13 days and mourn in mass, read Quran, recite marsiyahs and verses in honour of Husain. With the act of charity the Muharram celebrations end.

38. Glory of Goddess Mahalakshmi
In the month of 'Margasir' (Nov-Dec), on every Thursday Goddess Mahalakshmi is worshipped with utmost devotion by women. Thursay is the auspicious day for worshipping Mahalakshmi who as per Hindu belief is the embodiment of all wealth and food materials.

39. Blooming New Moon (Bakul Amabasya)
On new-moon day of Pausha (December), the festival of worshipping the sacred mango tree with offerings of special cake is celebrated. Mango, the king of fruits bloom in this season to bear mangoes in the ensuing spring season. In temples, festivals and religious observances; the branches of mango tree are utilized to generate holiness, purity and sanctity.

40. Christmas
The festival of Christmas celebrates the birth of **Jesus Christ on 25th December** and conveys his message of love, tolerance and brotherhood. Fun, frolic, and laughter mark this year-end festival. Jubilation, parties and gaiety continue till the New Year.

WELLNESS BY
OUR
BELIEFS & CUSTOMS

Mystical Customs

Hair-parting: As a religious rite in some part of our society, the husband is asked to perform this after the marriage. Wife is made to sit in a comfortable place, parts her hair from the centre and the husband puts a red mark with vermilion as a symbol of married woman. It is also to ward off evil spirits and to make her look beautiful. A woman especially in her pregnancy is subjected to attacks of evil spirits. The religious intention of the rite is to bring about prosperity to the mother and long life to the unborn child.

Carrying a child: In rural India people observe certain hygienic conditions as social rites such as pregnant woman should always sit at a comfortable clean place, wear clean clothes, eat good food, bathe in warm water mixed with medicinal herbs, avoid excessive exercise, excessive daytime sleep and avoid long excited talks, arguments, angers, evade awakening at night, always be busy with good things and remain happy. The husband should always fulfil the wishes of the pregnant wife, as it will bring good luck and health to the unborn child and wife.

Intellectual Wellbeing: After the birth of a child, hymns are uttered for production of intelligence or for intellectual wellbeing of the child. They are recited with the great **Gayatri Mantra:**

"Om Bhur Bhuvah Swaha Tat Savitu Varenyam. Bhargo Devasya Dhimahi Dhiyo Yo Nah Prachodyaat."
Om (means Brahma, Vishnu, Mahesh) Bhur (earth) Bhuvah (sky) Swaha (heaven) Tat (the essence) Savitu (the creator—divine light—sun)

Varenyam (is worth worshipping) Bhargo Devasya Dhimahi (upon the glory we meditate) Dhiyo Yo Nah Prachodyaat (the intellect which may guide us)

It means—"Let us meditate on the most excellent light of the Creator (the divine Sun); may the Almighty guide our intellect and illuminate our minds."

The substances, with which the child is fed, are also conducive to mental health. The father with his fourth finger and with an instrument of gold gives honey and ghee (clarified butter) to the child. The formula employed Bhurbhuvah swaha (putting into mouth everything good for intellect and well being).

Ayusha (Longevity): The next spiritual ceremony called Ayusha or the rite for ensuring strength, martial, healthy, pure and long life for the child is performed by the father through a priest.

Sasthi: On 6th day of birth of child a spiritual activity named as 'Sasthi' puja takes place in the house where the child is born. Few neighbouring women are called for performing worship to the goddess 'Sasthi'. They form portrait of the goddess by placing few 'Cowries' on the inside wall of the house. The goddess is worshipped and a special cake (Pitha) called 'Chakuli' made of the rice paste and pulses is prepared and offered as "Prasad" to the goddess.

Name-giving: On the age of 21st day of the child, worship of Lord Satyanarayana is performed in the house for the well being of the child. The priest with his team arrives in the evening and performs the ceremony. As per ritual on this auspicious day, the maternal uncle arrives with new belongings such as new mattress, pillow, mosquito net, cradle, golden chain, golden ring, silver bracelet and new dresses for the baby. Family members also receive new dresses.

This ceremony is then celebrated to give names to the child, usually two names; one is the popular one and the other being a patronymic or matronymic. It is believed that a link exists between name and deeds or course of life of the divine or a human being. Therefore, a good name represents goodness, inspires respect and strength. In olden days people use to prefer god's names but now modern names are aesthetic in sense, and tend to be neither too long nor too short. After the ceremony is over, the priest is offered with presents and gifts. Alms are distributed to the poor people.

First Outing (Nishkramana): Every step in the life of the child is a festive occasion for the parents and the family, and it is celebrated with appropriate religious ceremonies. Usually forty days after the birth of the child or on the fourth month after the birth, the child is taken out of the house and is introduced to the outer world. Therefore, gods are worshipped for the health, development, well being and protection of the child from evil eye. The child is taken to the temple for blessing.

First Feeding (Annaprashana): Feeding the child with solid food is the next important stage in the life of the child. While the quantity of the mother's milk diminishes, the child requires solid food. This ceremony is connected with the physical need of the child at six or seven months. Food being a life giving substance has something mysterious from which life emanates. The source of energy is to be infused into the child with the help of gods. Praise of food is found in the Vedas and the Upanishads and they are sung during the first feeding of the child. The food with different kind of flavours, 'Kheer' (frumenty) is cooked for the child to eat.

As a custom, the maternal uncle sends new utensil / vessel with new dresses to the nephew / niece. The child wears the new dresses and takes food served in the new utensil / vessel given by maternal uncle. At least seven or more children from the neighbourhood are invited and fed in the house. A prayer is offered that all the senses of the child be gratified and he/she may live a happy and contended life.

Mother's Protégé: In popular belief of Indian society, it is said that if any person gets attracted to a cute, healthy child by its appearance, the child suffers from fever and become unwell. It is taken as if the evil sight of someone has affected the baby. There is a custom in families to avoid such bad impact of evil spirits and evil sights.

The mother wears black collyrium (Kajal) in her own eyes and also applies to the kid's eyes. She takes some 'Kajal' from her own eyes with her finger and applies the same either behind the ear of the child or on the right side forehead of the child forming a 'Tika'(circular mark) in order to keep the child protected from evil effects of wicked persons / spirits. This practice is followed everyday.

If a child has fever, becomes dull and always cries; it is felt that bad effect has come from somebody's evil eye or evil desire. To cure him; ladies in the family bring 5 or 7 or 9 red chillies. Holding those in closed palm the lady or the mother rolls her hand over the child from head to toe. After this, the chillies are burnt in fire. The child gets cured and comes back to full vigour.

Tonsure (Mundan Ceremony): Cutting the hair is essential to keep head clean. According to medical book, shaving &cutting the hair and nails, remove impurities and gives delight, freshness, prosperity, happiness and beauty to the body. Tonsure ceremony is also connected to the idea of health and beauty of the child. Some people perform this ceremony at the end of the first, third, fifth or seventh year after the birth of child. It is always performed during the day time. Its performance in the even-year is prohibited. Mundan ceremony in the third year is regarded very propitious. An auspicious day is fixed for the ceremony and lord Ganesh is worshipped on this day with distribution of food to the poor and to the Brahmins. The mother who gave birth to the child takes the child in her lap who wears new clothes for the occasion for Mundan. The prayers cited in the ceremony are meant for the long life of the child.

Piercing the ears (Karnavedha): Ear piercing was ornamental in its origin but later on, ancient-doctors suggested it useful for preventing Hernia and some other ailments. It is recommended that ears of every child should be pierced for protection, and it becomes a part of religious ceremony so that the chances of some diseases may be minimised. The idea of piercing in early age of the child is to make it easier and less troublesome to the child. Gold, silver or iron needles are used in piercing ears. The right ear of the boy and left ear of the girl is pierced first. After piercing, oil is applied to the ears. At the end, presents are exchanged and guests, priests are entertained.

Protective Horse-Shoe: When small kids of age 4 to 9 years have abrupt awakening from deep sleep and they cry; then the mother tries to make him/her sleep. It happens several times during sleep. Parents consult some mentors and local experts for remedy. One unique practice is then followed.

As per advice of such persons, they collect one horse-shoe i.e. U-shaped iron plate from a horse's hoof and few hairs of horse. The mother keeps these under the child's pillow before sleep. The child sleeps resting his head on this pillow. The iron piece is kept regularly under the pillow till he is grown up and fully cured.

It is a popular belief that by possessing iron piece one can repel evil soul and it cannot come closer. The horse shoe made of iron that is worn by the horse travels difficult terrains with high speed and crushes all obstacles, is a symbol of courage and dynamism and therefore is believed to protect the child.

Learning of Alphabets (Vidya Arambha): In earlier times the education of children began with the memorising of the sacred hymns. After the art of writing started in India, the ceremony of learning of alphabets started. At the age of four or five years when the child is prepared to receive education, he is taught the alphabets. On an auspicious day the child is bathed, and Lord Ganesh, goddess Saraswati, family deity and other deities are worshipped. This rite consists of both writing and reading and salutation to Saraswati, Narayan and Lakshmi. The child is made to read the written words thrice. The teacher is presented gifts.

Ensuring Goodluck

There is popular belief in India that Amulet, Metallic Bracelet, Necklace, Ring, Talisman prepared out of God-worshipping with sacred chanting does acquire magical spiritual power. In order to get protected from dangers arising out of ill effects of evil souls, bad influence of wicked persons and adverse impact of stars; people wear these around their waist, neck, arms, wrist, fingers etc in a way that these touch the body to bring the desired result.

Parents make their child wear such talisman designed out of a small round copper metal or even using one paisa round old copper coin. The centre hole of the coin is tied to a black rope which is wrapped around child's waist. This is supposed to be endowed with magic powers averting evil and bringing good luck to the child.

Further, one amulet or a metal charm made of copper is made on order by the village blacksmith. It is designed in the form of a small cylindrical tube with one end open, other end closed and a round hook on its centre. It is then given to local Exorcist (Ojha) for making it as a talisman. Putting inside some herbs through its open end, he closes it. This is then worshipped before God by his chanting of prayers. The Exorcist is famous in art of exorcism and making such sacred amulet/talisman, which is a charm against evil. This is tied by a black thread around the upper arm of the child for his wellbeing.

AYURVEDIC PRACTITIONER

In rural India, treatment for illnesses are invariably taken by all the villagers from Kabiraj / Vaidya who treats by Ayurvedic methods. Some teachers of primary school are also famous Kabiraj of villages. He is always called home to check up and prescribe medicines when any one suffers from ill health.

The Kabiraj prescribes some of the famous medicines which are popularly known as 'Makardhwaj', 'Mahashankh', 'Panchan' etc. He visits home and checks physically, counts pulse and observes body temperature by touching and feeling. He advises rest and light food like Barley, Saboodana, fruits and liquid diet etc.

In case of severity, he prepares 'Panchan' by boiling several herbs which are essential to heal a particular suffering / disease. This boiled water is taken by the patient 3-4 times a day for few days to get cured. His treatment and medicines are effective as people get cured very fast.

Diseases such as fevers, cold, cough, inflammations, digestive disturbances, skin eruptions, wounds are treated by him. He cures by both Naturopathy and Ayurvedic methods. His prescriptions utilising leaves of holy basil, cardamom, fenugreek, ginger, garlic, turmeric (Haldi), myrobalan (bahera), raisins, almonds, onion, lemon, aniseed, fruit pulps, long pepper, honey etc are sure cure for various illnesses. He advises well balanced diets, sufficient physical exercise, fresh air, plenty of sunlight, cleanliness, therapeutic bath, adequate rest and right mental attitude for ensuring proper health and preventing disease.

Trio-Myrobalans: Taking advice from the Kabiraj (Vaidya), parents follow an ayurvedic practice to make the child hale and hearty, free from cough, cold and stomach disorder. They feed Trifala-water to the child every morning. They soak Trifala in water kept in a stone-pot at evening. Trifla consists of Harad (Chebulic myrobalan), Bahera (Belliric myrobalan), and Amla (Emblic myrobalan). Every morning a glass of this water is given to drink. The taste is bitter and one may refuse to take it. With lot of persuasion, mothers can succeed in feeding the child, after which they can take breakfast. It is learnt that children who take this regularly gain good health and physique.

COMMENCEMENT CEREMONY

This is a function which a very few people perform. A child undergoes the rituals of beginning of learning at the tender age before he is admitted to any formal schooling. In previous chapter, Karnavedha (ear-piercing) has been covered but later on in our society, to formally maintain the ritual, the ceremony of "Bidya-Arambha" (beginning of learning) and ceremony of "Karnavedha" (ear-piercing) are performed together by affluent people. Although the child is admitted to school, the father performs it as a spiritual rite to initiate learning by scriptural methods and obtains heavenly blessings.

At the age of about 7 years parents perform this for their child. On that auspicious day the child is made to get up early and finish morning activities. A marriage stage is decorated inside the courtyard. Earthen water pot with mango leaves, coconut, paddy, vermilion, turmeric (Haldi), cloth, towel etc are brought and kept according to the instructions of the priest. Invited relatives, neighbours and family friends sit around the stage. The child is bathed in turmeric water. Then he is made to wear a long white cotton cloth (Dhoti) like an adult man even though he is a child. He is also made to wear a sacred thread by the priest and remains bare bodied. He looks like a tender Brahmin pundit or a Gurukul student.

Then the ear-piercing ceremony starts. The village-barber shaves hair from his head. The barber becomes ready to pierce his ear by a needle. The Priest chants some hymns loudly. One person comes with a pot of molasses (Gud) and approaches the child. He then advises the child to eat the molasses and look towards the direction of maternal uncle's house to perhaps divert the child's attention on the pain of piercing the ear. When the child is ready with all such positioning, at that time the barber pierces the right ear followed by the left ear. The child feels minimal pain during this activity. Both the ears are tied with small threads anointed with turmeric (Haldi) and vermilion (Sindur) paste.

The invited preceptor (Kul Guru), a Brahmin pundit who is the preceptor for the dynasty is given respectful welcome to the ceremony. His activities start next. The child is first blessed by him and then he accompanies the child to one secluded place. The Guru comes closer to the ears of the child covering head and face of both of them by a cloth / visor. Now the Guru uder this visor infuses into the child's ear by sounding the 'Maha Mantra' (Great Hymn) in low voice i.e.

"HareKrishna HareKrishna Krishna Krishna Hare Hare.
HareRama HareRama Rama Rama Hare Hare".

He whispers and advises the child saying: "Every day you must utter this as prayer and practice regularly. I am passing this to you secretly as a powerful great hymn 'Maha Mantra' and do not reveal this hymn openly to anybody." Now a day, this hymn is widely known and uttered openly with devotion for the welfare of the humanity. Once upon a time, this was a secret powerful hymn whispered by a Guru.

The ceremonial function then starts on the stage with chanting of sacred words for long hours by Priests / Pundits. After ceremonial Puja, a fire oblation (Havan) is performed. The child sits in the Puja near to the priest and follows the directions of the Priest. The child has to break 108 coconuts. Being a kid, he formally breaks one or two coconuts, and then touches the rest to the hitting stone. His father stands beside him and breaks those one after another on behalf of him. The Astrologer (Jyotish), The Priest, The Pundits and The Kul Guru all chant some words of hymn.

After the occasion is over, a grand feast (meal) is served to all invited guests, pundits, the neighbours, villagers and poor people and tramps of the society.

This is the manner the Commencement Ceremony (Bidya Arambha) and ear-piercing ceremony (Karnavedha) are celebrated with induction of 'Maha Mantra'.

Initiation

(Upanayana / Janeo)

Upanayana ceremony performed before marriage is called 'Janeo ceremony' (sacred thread ceremony). It means the rite through which a man is initiated into the vows of the Guru, the Vedas, the restrains, observances and the vicinity of a God. The most auspicious Lord Ganesha is propitiated and several other Goddesses, Sri Lakshmi, Dhriti, Medha, Pushti, Shradha and Saraswati are worshipped. This rite marks that the youth has to lead a systematic and more responsible life thence onward.

Generally white thread is used in Janeo (thread ceremony). Some people believe that Janeo forms a magical barrier; when used as a ring neck let, a magical circle keeping off evil influences and preventing the dissipation of good forces. It is also a symbol of more responsible life. Before the ceremony the boy is regarded as once-born and after the ceremony he becomes Dwija (twice-born), and is admitted to the privileges of his society and has access to the sacred books.

The sacred thread is usually worn over the left shoulder, going diagonally across the chest, and under the right arm to the right hip. There are three threads in Janeo remind a young man of the Pranava (OM, the symbol of Absolute) Medha (intelligence) and Shradha (diligence), the three essential guides for education and the life of a householder.

The boy is taught the most sacred Gayatri Mantra (hymn) or the worship of the Sun so that he may absorb its brilliance and effulgence.

VENERATION TO LORD SATYANARAYAN

Parents perform Satyanarayan Puja (worshipping of Lord Narayan) every year on the child's birth day. The family priest performs this Puja at their house. Satyanarayan is Lord Bishnu; his photo is kept on a small stool decorated by peacock wings, garlands, whole bunch of ripe bananas.

The child is made to sit in this Puja (worshipping). The priest chants hymns and welcomes the Gods with austerity and directs the child to follow his actions as the Priest demonstrates. Without understanding the meaning of chanting, the meaning of activities, postures and offerings, the child is asked to follow the priest with a sacred mind of devotion and concentration on the Lord. The "Prasad" (food offering to God) in this occasion are always crushed ripe banana, crushed coconut, powdered flour or powdered rice with sweet milk named as "Sirni" in eastern India.

Then the priest with his group performs a chorus named as "Pala" i.e. an episode of Lord Satyanarayan described in melodious devotional rhythm along with musical instruments such as Tabor (Mridang), Cymbal (Jhanja) and 'Clappings'. These episodes are written in 'Pala-Book' according to the age of the child. The function takes 2 hours to complete with 1 hour of 'Puja'. The story is about an event depicting powerful influence of God Satyanarayan who protects a distressed person/ family from the sufferings in miraculous manner. All the family members and neighbours assemble, sit down and listen attentively with devotion.

At the end, the Sirni-"Prasad" is served to all those who are present in the 'Puja' and 'Pala'. Next day early morning this "Prasad" is distributed to all houses of the relatives, neighbours and kith and kin.

This 'Puja' is for all-round development and good health of the child. Sometimes this is done few days after the birth-day. The 'Puja' is performed by normal families. But the 'Puja' followed with the 'Pala' with playing of instruments and devotional songs are attractive and are only performed by affluent people in the society. In rural places, the families and neighbours love this devotional group-rhythm and listen with full attention to the Lord's glory.

The Priest is offered with gift money (Dakshina), new cloth and dresses as per the capability of the house owner. The priest showers blessings by uttering sacred words and pouring raw rice—granules on the heads of all the family members and leaves the house.

Kids' Gratification

(Bal Lila)

I t is said; children are symbol of purity and godliness. Children's satisfaction and blessings are the greatest spiritual blessings. Some affluent parents on every birth day of their child arrange "Kids' Gratification" (Bal Lila) in the local temple for prosperity and good health of the child. This is a secluded auspicious place with spiritual atmosphere. The priest of the temple conducts this function of 'Bal Lila'.

'Bal Lila' is the invitation to all kids 4 years to 12 years age of the locality to attend a morning feast at the temple on the occasion of the particular child's birthday. Person on behalf of the child visits every house of the locality or the village on the previous day and verbally invites their children to attend such morning feast to be served at the temple.

The previous night parents remain busy in despatching their materials, articles, big kitchen-pots, cooking hardware etc to the temple. Rice, Dal (lentil) cooking ingredients and vegetables are sent to the temple. Early morning on the very day, the Chef, family members with helpers arrive at the temple and make arrangements for cooking and dining. Simple items are prepared such as Rice, Pulse (Dalma), Vegetarian Curry (Sabji), sour preparation/Chutney and sweet rice-porridge (Kheer). These are offered to the temple God as "Prasad" and then ready for serving to the children.

Children arrive in early morning at about 06.30 Hrs to 07.30 Hrs in groups with escorts and guardians. Hundreds of children flock there at this specified time. They are made to sit down by batches on the cemented open courtyard of the temple. Leaf plates usually of green banana or plate of dry leaves are placed in front of each child for serving food. The parents and relatives of the child take care of the invited kids and serve food on their plates. The kids take food with satisfaction. At the end of feast of every batch, children are asked to stand up. The priest tells them to utter in chorus, by following and repeating his words. The children repeat this in a chorus. The meaning of those words is their prayer to God for wellness and all-round prosperity of the child whose birthday is celebrated. Then they wash their hands, mouth and go back to their school or home. Several batches take food and repeat the above prayer. Beggars, distressed people and outsiders are then given food. At the end the priest, cook, volunteers etc take food. All of them in batches after finishing their food utter the same prayer-cum-blessings and leave their seats. The entire celebration comes to an end. Then the courtyard is washed and all the hardwares, articles, cooking utensils are cleaned and taken back.

Some committed parents as a sacred vow continue to perform this on every birthday of their son or daughter even if they are grown up, adult and aged.

Chorus Of Rhythmic Chants

(Asta Prahari)

'Asta Prahari' is a nonstop rhythmic mass chanting of Lord Krishna for 8 Prahars (32 hrs). This is spiritual celebration of continuously uttering God's name by a group of devotees without stop. The method was devised by the famous spiritual person Shri Shri Chaitanya Mahaprabhu of Nadiya Navdweep of Assam. Now-a-days ISCON is the follower of this tradition.

The entrance courtyard in front of the house where the function should take place is cleaned and decorated. The roof is temporarily covered mostly by bamboo long-sticks, coconut leaves and boughs or by cloth for protecting from dust, heat and sun rays. The soil of the yard is washed and mopped by sacred cow dung water and left to dry up. Coloured flags, coloured paper of different style and design are cut for decoration. The poles, bars and the stage are decorated with such coloured papers.

At the centre of the courtyard, a stage (Mandap) under the roof is made. A coloured cotton cloth called 'Shamiana' is spread over the centre stage as its roof. The Mandap is made by placing stools in pyramid form and are covered by white cloth. Big size framed photographs of various Gods, specially of Krishna, Narayan, Nitai-Gaur, Shiva, Chaitenya, Jagannath, Shriram, Radhakrishna are placed all 4 sides of these stools in tier over the tier.

Then flower decoration starts. Garlanding of each God's photo is done. Then the stage and the 'Mandap' are decorated by flower garlands.

Evening to night, Decoration continues from evening to night. Lighting decoration is also done in the courtyard and on the stage.

An expert priest for conducting 'Asta Prahari' is invited. He arrives on the first day and continues up to the third day i.e. the end of the function. One base group of devotees are invited from the locality to start the Puja on the first day. The 1st day is called 'Adhibasa' in which Puja starts after the midnight and in early morning.

At morning 03.30 Hrs, a group of devotees carry empty earthen pot/ pitcher (Kalash) and walk to the nearest canal or river. They take bath and fill the 'Kalash' with water. These Kalash are established in the centre stage of 'Asta Prahari'. While bringing water the priest does some worshipping and chanting. A clay lamp with ghee and cotton is lit and kept inside a big earthen pot with earthen cover. The body of the pot has small perforations or holes to allow oxygen for continuous burning.

At about 04.30 hrs welcome Puja of Lord Krishna is done. Thus God's arrival on the centre-stage, takes place. The devotional singing of Lord's name starts continuously by repetition. The base group of people doing this 'Adhibasa' initiate such singing. The group in chorus always recite the sacred names of Lord Krishna in form of rhythmical music along with instrument of Tabor, Cymbal etc while walking around the centre stage in clock wise direction.

Devotional words of name-dropping are recited and sung in rhythm. These words are also written or painted prominently on a board by fixing at the entrance and displaying to the devotees, visitors and public. The new invited chorus group of devotees are reminded by this display to get prepared to sing and recite after joining the devotional chorus called as 'Samkirtan'.

The name-repetition was done with melodious tunes by the group. The group leader first sings one line; others repeat and follow the rhythm. The leader after few minutes changes the rhythm. It is very attractive, devotional and full of emotions. Anybody from the locality, neighbours and families is free to join the chorus of repeatedly singing god's name in pleasure. At least, four to five groups of devotees are invited to arrive at the function and join the chorus. From day time up to evening, these groups come by batches. After they arrive at the entrance of 'Ashta Prahari', they seek to systematically enter by starting the singing (Samkirtan) there. They begin their singing parallel with the previous group among their group with instruments and slowly merge in, then the previous group stops and goes to take rest. In this manner, group after group join the chorus, thus continuous rhythm of reciting God's name never stops and continues flawlessly without break and interruption. The Puja in morning, mid day and waving of light (Aarti) at evening are done by the Priest. The food arrangement, sleeping and rest arrangements all are provided by the head of the house.

The 2nd day of Astaprahari is called 'Nama Yajna'. Non-stop chanting goes on group by group full day and night. The 3rd day is the completion day, called 'Nagar Kirtan' means singing devotional song in the locality approaching every house. All groups together travel from ward to ward, house to house singing the God's name. House owners', families receive the 'Name-dropping'(Kirtan) in front of their house, come out, offer some money, fruits, sweets etc as gift (Dakshina) according to their interest and option. At noon, the groups return back to the place of 'Asta Prahari'.

Now the concluding ceremony of 'Asta Prahari' happens. The sacred book of Astaprahari is read with rhythm by the Priest. Others follow & repeat. An earthen pot with curd-water with Turmeric (Haldi) paste is prepared; a bunch of mango leaf is kept inside. The person for whom the 'Asta Prahari' has been reserved is decorated by besmearing him with sandal paste, turmeric paste (Haldi) on the body & fore head. A cloth is wrapped as a turban on his head. The earthen pot with curd water cum turmeric is kept on the turban-head.

He walks around the stage carrying the pot on the head. Holding the pot on the head by left hand, he takes one bunch of mango leaf in right hand and dips it into the curd-water. Then he waves the bunch of leaves towards the public (audience) by throwing the sacred droplets of curd water of the Lord over them and purifying the common mass. This, "Nama-Yajna" i.e. singing sacred names of God along with playing of instruments like Tabor (Mridanga), Cymbals (Jhanja) and the chorus voice of the public continues by moving around the centre stage several times.

This moment is heart touching. The spectators weep and sob with tears rolling down from their eyes. This may be out of extreme devotion to Lord Krishna and for their heartfelt prayer and blessing to the person carrying the sacred pot.

At the end of such 'Samkirtan' the priest does a great chorus of devotional and musical rhythm and thrills the ambience when he instructs all to dance remembering God in heart with deep devotion and advises to break the earthen pot by throwing on the ground. The pot breaks and the curd cum turmeric water flows down on the ground. Immediately everyone rolls down on the moist ground of turmeric-curd-water and love to besmear the whole body. This tradition has originated by the great spiritual preceptor, 'Chaitanya Dev'. Thus the 'Asta Prahari' comes to an end.

All invited people and the audience are fed with a good vegetarian meal as "Prasad" of 'Asta Prahari'.

This is a great tradition of devotional path of singing, repeating god's name. The words of name-droppings (Samkirtan) may vary but the celebration remains the same. This continues in most places of eastern India (Bihar, Odisha, Jharkhand & North East States). In Krishna temples, ISCON temples, Jagannath temples and community places 'Asta Prahari' is always performed with deep devotion and dignity. Also people perform it at their own house for well being of their family or by keeping vow / reserve in the name of their child for his prosperity.

DEITY'S VISION

'Marjana'of a Deity (the Goddes) is the morning vision (Darshan) and the morning bath by holy water of sandal paste, vermilion, scented oil, wearing of new clothes, garlanding and then 'Archana' by burning scented sticks, ghee lamps etc. People perform this normally in the temple, before village goddess and their presiding deity.

First tradition is to arrive at the temple, wash hand, feet, face etc and get purified in the big water pond of the temple. Then people come inside, search for their Priest (the Panda). The temple Priest arrives and accompanies to the shop selling "Prasad" where Sweets, Coconut, Bangles, Sari, flower Garland, and Earthen ghee lamp are purchased. The devotee offers 12 or 16 hand-length of black or red coloured sari to the goddess. The sari is given for wearing over the deity. The Priest then guides the devotee to enter the temple. He makes bathing of the goddess applying oil, sandal paste, turmeric paste and perfume on the body of the Deity. Then the Sari is covered over the Goddess. The devotee worships the Deity by touching the pulpit of the Deity and bowing down before her. The "Prasad" is offered by the Priest to the Goddess then the devotee walks around the temple and visits other Gods in the side temples. The devotee sits on the floor of the inside courtyard of the temple and prays for some time.

The evening episode is more interesting. People visit the temple for evening prayer and vision (Darshan) of the Goddess. The evening adoration of the Goddess by waving lamp (Aarti) before her with beating of drum, gong (Ghanta), blowing of conch, trumpet etc are very attractive and creates a perfect devotional ambience. One gets sentimental, purified, and god-loving and becomes ardent devotee at that moment. After finish of activities of worship, adoration of the Deity, waving of lamp with music; devotees are permitted to enter inside up to the holy image and offer their obeisance there. The Priest is offered with gift of money for offering Puja and making the holy vision of the goddess by the devotee.

There are festivals at the temple on auspicious days of a year like Sankranti, Astami etc. Heavy rush of public occurs on these days.

SOCIAL INVOCATION TO LORD

Worship of Lord Shiva (Panchanan) takes place in local community or village by group of neighbouring houses. Common places like crossroads, village-roads of the locality are chosen in open air by group of neighbours to observe a small spiritual fair called as **'Mela'** for celebrating worship of Lord Shiva. Different places about four to five locations are selected in the locality where reasonable numbers of neighbouring families assemble for such fair. This traditional worship originates from a belief that such worship harnesses welfare for the society. Every year for 5 days from Dussehra day to full moon day, this worship is celebrated. Each day is dedicated to one family. Allotment of day is from 1st to 5thday and is fixed against every family. Therefore in very systematic manner every year the families take automatic initiative on particular day. Any family wishing to perform his 'Mela' but un-allotted against these days can also do the same. He is accommodated during these days on any day by allotting additional worship (Mela) after completion of first allotted worship (Mela).

The school going children of every family get involved in this Mela. Parents advise their children to organize this community-worship by assembling and arranging the function in a team. They clean the ground, garbage, cut the growth of wild grass and level it by contributing their own physical labour. Mothers and elderly ladies in every house initiate the activity by involving their own children and guide them how to perform the fair.

The family / house on his allotted day of worship sends the members / children with all utensils, brass lamp, pots, worshipping articles etc. These articles are first washed in the nearby water pond or canal. They collect flower, cloth, leaves, tender grass, raw rice, paddy, sandal wood, vermilion, camphor, tinkling bells, gong, conch etc and all other worshipping ingredients as prescribed by the priest and advised by the mother. The Mela of worshipping Lord Shiva starts around 20:00 Hrs and continues for more than 1 hour. All neighbouring family members gather at Mela and sit down with devotion. They listen to the Priest's loud recitation of God's glory. People blow conch, ring the bell, the gong etc during the worship. In the middle of worship as per the guidance of Priest, sounding of God's name in chorus called as 'Hari Bol' and 'Namah Shivay' are uttered by all the devotees from time to time. The Mela comes to an end followed by distribution of "Prasad" to all. The "Prasad" is unique and is called 'Panchamrit' made out of mixture of milk, curd, banana, ghee & honey and is quite tasty as well as hygienic. It gives enough pleasure, encouragement to the families as they celebrate this sacred community-Puja late evening after finishing their day's hard work and returning from cultivating field. The speciality of the function is inducting the future generation (children) in to devotional path, physically involving them, adopting team work and organizing for welfare of the society.

ADORED PRECEPTOR

(Guru)

In Indian society, there are number of adored preceptors (Guru) who are accepted by families as their mentor. They are popular among certain groups of people who follow such Preceptors (Gurus), their principles and worship them as God-man. Some of them deliver moral precepts, religious teachings, mythological stories from epics, philosophy from Vedas, Vedanta and Upanishads in public forum.

Such preceptor (Guru) is adored by families and most of the villagers in the locality. People used to totally surrender before this revered Guru. They consult him for all their life's incidents, troubles and solutions. They believe that the spiritual power of Guru can resolve all their problems and he is powerful enough to derive God's blessings for the well beings of his devotees.

This preceptor stays in a monastery (Mutt) made for his living where he has the worship-room, guest rooms, assembly place for mass prayer etc. His disciples and fellow followers live there. They take care of the Guru, the monastery as well as the devotees visiting the place for holy vision of the Guru and make their transit stays. The devotees from distant places come there to worship the Guru and the presiding deity of the monastery and listen to his discourse.

On auspicious Hindu festive days, like Rasleela, duet of Radha Krishna, birthday of Krishna (Janmastami), Shivratri, Dusshera, Diwali, Holi etc grand celebrations take place in such hermitage/monastery. Devotees glorify the Guru by religious, melodious prayers playing the musical instruments with devotional dance. The Guru is worshipped by people as a "God". The propitiatory food offered to him and the presiding deity of the Mutt during worship is called "Prasad" which is distributed to all devotees. All devotees whoever visit the monastery usually carry some offerings in form of money or material. They prefer to stay few days to participate in mass prayer and the worshipping of the Guru. Food is served on behalf of the monastery to all. One after another, they meet the Guru in person, pay homage to Him and deliver their personal matters to Him. After they offer their last obeisance and obtain his touch, his blessings and guidance; they depart.

In several occasions, wishing his auspicious presence, devotees invite him to their house, their villages, social functions, have mass prayer, worship him, inaugurate their new activities and perform opening ceremonies by his sacred hands. He is invited to a grand stage for delivering spiritual discourses where hundreds of people arrive to listen to him. He then performs mass prayer with musical instruments in public. People get thrilled and enjoy the group rhythmic prayer (Bhajan). Some devotees get emotional and dance with devotion during the melodious mass prayer. It becomes a very amusing, ambience filled with spiritual sentiments of praising God.

At present these preceptors have educational institutions, hospitals, temples, meditation centres, yoga centres, discourse halls, community services, inns, boarding houses etc in their premises for the benefit of the public. There are millions of devotees as members who contribute donations, gifts etc. Such establishments are very rich and are doing some benevolent social activities. There are several spiritual TV channels where they often deliver discourses and demonstrate mass prayers. Some of such trusts and preceptors serve the society by contributing medical treatments, providing medical awareness, teaching and demonstrating Yoga and meditation techniques.

Pilgrimage To A Notable Shrine

(Jagannath Puri)

There are several reputed shrines in India such as Jagannath Puri, Badri Nath, Dwarka, Rameshwaram, Kashi Vishwanath, Shirdi, Tirupati, Vaishno Devi, Ajmer and Golden Temple etc. As per popular Indian belief, visiting these shrines for a Darshan (Vision of Deity) bring salvation to life. Pilgrimage to Lord of the Universe, Jagannath at Puri is one such unique experience that has been described here.

Puri is situated on the sea shore on the Bay of Bengal at a distance of 60 Kms from Bhubaneswar, the capital city of the state Odisha. It is well connected by road, rail and air. It is the aboard of Lord 'Jagannath' or the 'Lord of the Universe' or the 'Supreme Personality of the universe'. Since time immemorial, it has been attracting millions of devotees for a holy vision of the deities and specially for viewing the trinity lords on the chariots in the world famous Car-Festival (Rath Yatra).

Pilgrims reaching Puri usually stay in tourist lodge, traveller's inn (Dharmashala) and hotels with nominal charges. They are guided by 'Temple Pandas' (Priests) to visit the temple and have the holy glance of Lord Jagannath. They arrive at the eastern gate of the temple called as "Lion-Gate" (Singh Dwar), pray the God by touching the "Aruna Pillar" at that place. This pillar carries on top, the image of Aruna, the charioteer of Sun God. In the passage room adjacent to the Lion gate and in front of the pillar is a Deity (Image) of Lord Jagannath named as 'Patita Pavan' i.e. 'God for liberating down trodden'. Those who are not permitted inside the temple can offer obeisance by taking vision (Darshan) of Lord Jagannath.

Devotees then gradually step up of the sacred 22 steps of the temple. People also take holy touch of the stepping stones and sit down for a while. Some people as per their vow make the kids to sit or prostrate on the step with devotion. Some also offer obsequies in honour of their ancestors on these steps. Before entering the temple they purchase "Prasad", flower garland and earthen butter-lamps. The butter-lamp is lighted and waved by hand as offering to the Deities with devotion. To protect from heavy rush of gathering, the respective 'Panda' takes care of his devotees (customers) protecting them by encircling the devotees and slowly guiding to proceed inside the temple.

Main Temple: There are four major temples in the row named as **'Viman'** which is the main temple where **Lord Jagannath** is worshipped with brother **Balabhadra,** sister **Subhadra** and his defendant weapon **Sudarshan**. The dancing hall named as **'Natamandap' (Mukhasala)** is next to **'Viman',** housing the jewellery, clothes, bedroom etc for Lord Jagannath and where the dancing ladies known as **'Devdasi'** used to dance before the Lords by singing the famous **'Gita-Govinda'** of Poet and devotee Jayadev. The audience hall named as **'Jagamohan'** is next to the Natamandap (Mukhasala). The **'Garuda Pillar'** is situated in 'Jagamohan'. The offering hall named as **'Prasada Mandap'** next to the 'Jagamohan' is a spacious hall with sculptures and paintings of Lord Krishna. Huge ""Prasad"" offerings of all varieties are made to Lord Jagannath from here during the rites.

Gates (Dwar): The temple has four gates namely Eastern Gate called as **'Lion Gate' (Singha Dwar)** which is the main entrance. Southern Gate is called as **'Horse Gate'**; Western gate is called as **'Tiger Gate'** and Northern gate is called as **'Elephant Gate'**. All these gates are situated on the outer wall called as **'Meghanad Prachir'**. Worshipping the gates also is a part of the daily ritualistic service of the temple. Navagrah reliefs are carved on the architraves of all the gates.

After crossing the 'Lion's Gate', devotees enter the temple by stepping up the 22 steps, proceed into the temple and first reach at "Garuda-Pillar". The image of the famous bird Garuda who is known as

God Vishnu's carrier is situated on the top of this pillar. Everyone while touching the sacred pillar views the trinity-lord (Jagannath, Balbhadra, Subhadra) at a distance. Garuda is the famous devotee of Lord Vishnu (Jagannath) who always remains standing in folded hands praying before the God. People do have broad, clear glance of the three famous deities and pay their obeisance by prostrating on ground and touching heads on the floor. They further go closer into the temple and have close holy vision of the deities. Pandas offer holy water and basil leaves (Tulsi) to the devotees and touch the holy cane-stick on the heads as blessings.

The Panda takes the devotees to move around the temple visiting the 'KalpaBat', 'Mukti Mandap', 'Rohini Kund', 'Bimla Temple', 'Lakshmi Temple', 'Ganesh Temple', 'Hanuman Temple', 'Koili Baikunth' etc. They are taken to the temple of Goddess Bimla by offering earthen butter lamps. Goddess Bimla is celebrated as owner / proprietor of the Jagannath Temple premises. As per custom of the temple, "Prasad" offered to the Trinity-Lords is taken to be further offered to Goddess Bimla after which it is named as **Maha Prasad** (Lord's propitiatory food) of the temple. It is then allowed to be sold or distributed to the public. Goddess Lakshmi is embodiment of wealth and prosperity. The devotees then visit and pray to the Goddess Lakshmi with lighting and waving of earthen butter lamps. As per popular belief and established ritual; to have prosperity in life, pilgrims sit down for a while on the floors of the Lakshmi temple.

They visit other places like 'Koili Baikunth', **'Anand Bazar'** and grand kitchen house etc. Every day 56 variety of "Prasad" are offered to the Lord. "Prasad" offerings after being made to Lord Jagannath are offered to Goddess Bimala Devi in the temple precincts and then become "Maha Prasad". It is sold outside the sanctum sanctorum area but within the temple. It remains hot for a long time as it is kept in the same earthen pots which are used to cook it. "Maha Prasad" at 'Anand Bazar' comprises of cooked boiled rice, pulses(Dal), varieties of vegetarian curries free from onion and garlic, green leaf preparations, item of sour preparation and sweet-porridge (Kheer) etc are meant for lunch or dinner. These are available to purchase and everyone irrespective of caste and creed are permitted to sit down on the floor and dine can be purchased from any vendor. This Maha"Prasad" is very delicious, can be carried away or can be taken there by sitting on the floor of 'Anand Bazar'. Also various types of dry sweets / "Prasad"s are available in 'Anand Bazar' which can be purchased by people to eat there or can be taken away.

Rituals of Deities: The ritual systems of the temple are very reliable and complex involving a multitude of functionaries above 1000 spread over 100 categories. The rituals (Niti) of Jagannath can broadly be divided into three parts, (i) the daily, (ii) the occasional / periodical and (iii) the festive. The fixed rituals that are observed daily are of routine. Lord Jagannath, Sri Devi, Bhudevi and Sudarshan are worshipped by the same Priest whereas Lord Balbhadra and Goddess Subhadra are worshipped by two different Priests.

Daily Ritual: These rituals commence on about 5:00 AM and continue till midnight. At least thrice daily, the worships are done with 16 special offerings (Upacharas) and during other times of the day with 5 offerings (Upachar). They include in seriatim the 'Mangala Aarti' (Morning adoration) after opening of temple door, 'Mailama' (taking off the cloths and flowers of previous night), 'Tadapalagi' (Putting on towels), 'Abakasa' (Cleaning of teeth and bathing), 'Vesa' (Dressing). Then a public visit (Darshan) called 'Sahana Mela' is held, when people are allowed to proceed near to the Jewelled-Throne (Ratnavedi) the ceremonial throne of the Trinity-Lord. After 'Sahana Mela' the Deities again change their dresses. An oblation to the fire is performed in the kitchen (Rosa Homa) and the fire is used in all the hearths for cooking the food for the Deities. Then the worship of Sun-God (Surya Puja) and worship of the Guardian-Deities (Dwarpal Puja) are done. After this, the ""Prasad"" called 'Gopala Vallabha Prasada' is offered. Next comes morning breakfast called 'Sakala Dhupa' followed by the ""Prasad"" called 'Prasada Mandap Prasada' and the mid day lunch called 'Madhyahna Dhupa'. The Deities change dress at each meal time; after each meal, betel nut are offered and after the meals the Deities enjoy siesta / rest (Pahuda) by switching off the lights and closing the door.

Special / Occasional Rituals: Periodical rituals are observed on occurrence of some specific occasions like Ekadashi, Sankranti, Amabasya, Eclipse day, Nakshatra and also for some mishaps in the temple. On Ekadashi, temple servant scales to the top of the temple (200 Ft) after night fall and burns a lamp there amidst the loud cheers of thousands of spectators. On every Thursday Goddess Lakshmi is washed, dressed and decorated carefully for a union with Lord Vishnu in the form of Jagannath. On new-moon day the moving idols of Jagannath visit the Sea-God 'Varuna' said to be father of Lakshmi.

Purifying& Consecrating Rites: These rites are performed when either a dog enters into the temple premises or a dead body is discovered somewhere in the temple area or spilling of blood, sputum, urine etc are noticed.

Festive Rituals: There are various festivals observed during the year, some outside the temple like Bathing Festival (Snan Yatra), Car Festival (Rath Yatra), Ferrying Festival (Chandan Yatra) and some inside the temple like Swinging Ceremony (Jhulan Yatra) etc. Each of these festivals is performed in great grandeur and magnificence when thousands of devotees visit Puri for the same.

Car Festival (Rath Yatra): The Car Festival or Festival of Chariots (Rath Yatra) in the month of June-July attracts pilgrims and visitors from all over the world. The Deities are taken out from the temple precincts in an elaborate ritual procession to their respective chariots which are huge, colourfully decorated and are drawn by hundreds and thousands of devotees on the grand road (Bada Danda), the grand avenue to the Gundicha temple about 3 Kms away to the north. After a stay of 8 days the deities return by 'Bahuda Yatra' (Return Car Festival) to their abode at Sri Mandir. Normally, in all temples across the world, the Moving Idols as representative deities comes out of the sanctum for ritual journeys;

whereas here, the Presiding Deities itself come out of the sanctum for such journey.

On this occasion the chariots, the wheels, the ropes, the grand avenue all become one with Lord Jagannath himself. It is believed that the glimpse of the Lord in the chariot in dwarf form ensures emancipation, release from the bondage of birth and death. The concept of the chariot has been explained as: the body is the chariot and the soul is the Deity installed in the chariot, the wisdom acts as the charioteer to control the mind and thoughts. Rath Yatra is the grandest festival of magnificent splendour, full of spectacle, drama and colour, the festival is the living embodiment of synthesis of various tribes, folks and races with classical, formal and sophisticated elements of the socio-cultural-religious-ethos of Indian civilization.

The kitchen: The kitchen of Lord Jagannath is considered as a largest and biggest kitchen of the world. The length of the kitchen is 150 Ft, breadth is 100 Ft and height is 20 Ft. It consists of 32 rooms with 250 earthen ovens within these. Around 700 cooks called as **Suaras** and 400 assistants served here every day for preparing Lord's food. There are three types of hearths named as Anna Chulha, Ahia Chulha, Pitha Chulha. The fire of this kitchen is never put out and is known as **Vaishnava Agni** because it is a fire in the kitchen of Lord Jagannath who is Vishnu himself. It is believed that Mahalaxmi cooks in the kitchen herself. The required timber for cooking in the kitchen is provided by State Forest Corporation. The unique feature of the kitchen is the clay pots placed in a special earthen oven five in numbers one on the top of another. Yet the one of the top is cooked first. There are two wells named as 'Ganga' and 'Jamuna' are near the kitchen for the purpose of supplying water to the kitchen. The wells are more than 10 Ft in radius and 100 Ft in depth. The food in the temple kitchen is prepared in such pure way and deep devotion that great spiritual impact is felt.

Temple Attendants 'Sevak': For the performance of various rituals at temple, a large number of attendants of Deities known as 'Sevaks' have been employed on hereditary basis. Such temple attendants called as **'Chhatisa Nijoga'** is of 36 categories perform temple services. King of Puri is the first 'Sevak' of the Lord. There are officials heading different departments for the service of the temple and the Lord such as 'RajGurus', 'Pattajoshi Mahapatra', 'Bhitarachu Mahapatra', 'Talucha Mahapatra', 'Mudiratha', 'Purohita', 'Puja Panda', 'Puspalaka', 'Khuntia', 'Mekapa', 'Pratihari', 'Karana', 'Daita' and 'Devdasi'.

After the visit of main temple, other holy places and famous temples situated at Puri viz. Gundicha temple, SriLokanath temple, Sankaracharya Math, Indradyumna-Pond, reputed monasteries etc are visited by the devotees on the next day. In the evening, they visit the Puri seashore/sea beach, sit down on the sands, enjoy the winds and tides and take bath in the waves of water inside the sea. Sea-bath in early morning at sunrise is very attractive and enjoyable at Puri. This is the longest sea beach in India with very broad and wide sandy sea shore. The road in front of the temple is called **'Grand-Road'** (**Bada Danda**) and is extremely wide and broad to accommodate millions of devotees every day, especially during the auspicious car festival.

Holy Dip In Sacred River

Kumbh Mela: Kumbh Mela is the most significant Hindu spiritual gathering in India that comes once in every three years, revolving among four major Hindu pilgrims centre of India such as **Allahabad, Haridwar, Ujjain and Nasik**. Allahabad city of Uttar Pradesh known as **Prayag** is situated around a beautiful river Ganga, Yamuna and Saraswati. The most holy spot in Allahabad is the confluence of these three rivers called as **'Triveni Sangam'**. This is the ancient city of pilgrimage, the bathing Ghats are of main attraction as large numbers of people flock here every day to take bath in Ganga River. Thousands of pilgrims bathe here every January-February and once in every twelve years at Kumbh Mela, the world's largest gathering of pilgrims drawing millions to take holy dip in the confluence of the rivers. Ardh Kumbh Mela is held every six years in Allahabad. It is believed that holy dip in the river Ganges during the Kumbha and Ardh Kumbha gives liberation (Moksha or Nirvana).

Fairs are held periodically every twelve or six years in Allahabad where largenumber of devotees get together to commemorate the churning of the ocean by the Gods and Demons for obtaining nectar (Amrit). When the coveted **Kumbh** (Jar) of nectar was obtained and carried by four Gods to heaven, they were chased by demons round the earth. During this chase, the Gods had put the Jar of Nectar (Amrit Kalash) at four different places Prayag, Haridwar, Nasik and Ujjain where one of the drops of this nectar are believed to have spilled into the waters at Sangam in Allahabad, banks of river Ganga in Haridwar, coast of Godawari in Nasik and coast of Shipra in Ujjain. Sages, Saints and pilgrims started periodically to flock at these pilgrimages (Tirth) to celebrate this divine event by taking dips in the holy rivers. It is a unique event that blends religious and social features of Indian society. Astrologer believe that the water of holy Ganges attain nectar like properties during the Kumb Mela season.

Rituals: Devotees believe that simply by bathing in the Ganges, one is freed from his past sins and thus is eligible for liberation from the cycles of birth and death. Other activities include religious discussions, devotional singing, mass feeding of holy men and women and the poor and religious assemblies where doctrines are debated and standardized. Irrespective of all worldly barriers of caste, creed, region, the Kumbh Mela has yielded a mesmeric influence over the minds and the imagination of the ordinary India. Maha Kumbh is the largest human gathering in history for the single cause. This auspicious time and space is attended by millions of people on a single day. The saints (Sadhus) are seen clad in saffron sheets with ashes and powder dabbed on their skin per the requirements of ancient traditions. Some called Naga Sanyasis, may not wear any clothes even in severe winter.

Holy Dip on Makar Sankranti: As per scriptures on the day of Makar Sankranti taking bath and giving donation is considered significant. Ganga is considered as river of heaven and this has come to earth by religious austerity. On the day of Makar sankranti, river Ganga had dissolved into the ocean. Hence the virtue of bathing in Ganga on this day is much more than any other day. In Kolkata, lakhs of devotees on this day come to take bath in **Ganga Sagar**. The meaning of bath is purity and Satvik i.e. anything pure, positive and beneficial. On this day the Sun enters the Tropic of Cancer (**Uttarayan**) increasing the entity and property of Sun which enters into our body through the sun rays. This supernatural rays increase strength of our body and provide good health, hence to gain these rays, to purify our body and soul, there is a custom to take bath in the early morning, few hours before sunrise called as Sacred Time (Punya Kal). Other than **Makar Sankranti**, on few festivals like **Karthik Purnima, Magh Purnima, Ganga Dusshera, Moni Amavasya,** it is extremely fruitful to take bath in Punya Kal as on this day Gods and pilgrimages reside in water. It is believed that on such occasions taking bath at this time for the sake of full purity gives result like bathing in milk.

Holy Dip in Chandrabhaga: Magha Saptami day is auspicious for worshipping "Sun God" and taking bath in the sacred river "Chandrabhaga" flowing near the famous temple **Konark** in Odisha well known internationally as **'Black Pagoda'**. Large stone wheels, big elephants, gigantic sculptures, arts and beautiful poses of Odyssey dance carved on the temple structure are magnificent pieces of architecture and attract large number of tourists throughout the year.

Thousands of devotees visit the place on this day to take the holy dip. The story says Shri Krishna's son Shamba was suffering from leprosy and was cured on this day by taking bath in this river and worshipping the "Sun God" at this place. Temple Konark was built to worship **"Sun-God"** as Shamba was cured by his blessing. On this day worshipping of the statue of Sun and inauguration of the temple took place. It is believed that by seeing the rising Sun at Chandrabhaga on this day, people do not suffer from diseases, troubles and miseries.

The place is the meeting place of river Chandrabhaga and the ocean (Bay of Bengal) and is adjacent to a group of beautiful standing dense green "Tamarisk Trees". The atmosphere is very attractive and charming. There is always cool breeze blowing with natural music of unique rhythm from Tamarisk Trees. View of small jungle with these trees on the sands of the river meeting the ocean is panoramic and produces humming sound when air passes through their needle like leaves. The meeting point of the river with ocean is now filled with sand and water flows to the sea under the sand.

Auspicious moment of watching sunrise in big round golden shape from the eastern horizon up above the sea gives utmost pleasure. Then the devotees take bath in the river. Everyone after taking bath prays by standing inside the river water and taking water in folded palms and offering to the Sun-God. It becomes a beautiful scene of mass bathing, mass prayer and offering with folded hands to the Sun-God. Then all the pilgrims after changing clothes visit the Temple Konark where they worship the "Navagraha" (Nine Deities) along with the Sun. In the noon, the mid day Sun is again worshipped by all with offering of "Prasad". In the afternoon, the Setting-Sun is finally worshipped by all. Thus the Rising-Sun, Mid-day-Sun and the Setting-Sun is watched and worshipped by the devotees throughout this auspicious day. After setting of the Sun, the devotees gradually depart.

In Odisha, every year this day **(Magha Saptami)** is celebrated as auspicious and people visit the place to have holy glance of the Sun-God and holy dip in sacred **"Chandrabhaga"**.

HINDU MARRIAGE CEREMONY

Importance: Hindu marriage (Vivaha) is one of the major sacraments (Samskar) of life. It is binding not only in this life but also in the next life. It is a union of not only the bride and groom, but also their families. Customs and ceremonies of marriage differ from region to region and even from village to village, but hymns in Sanskrit chanted in marriage ceremonies are the same in all the parts of India. Amongst various castes and tribes of Hindus, different forms of marriage are to be seen from the simplest modes of mutual consent to many other forms of marriage. In many parts of rural India, there are marriage customs encouraging Hindus to marry within the caste, sect, tribe and race forbidding to marry outside. In developed cities, the civilized mass have undergone changes and celebrate inter caste marriages. Marriage receives great importance not only as a social necessity, but also a religious duty for everyone. It is considered that a man is incomplete without a wife. Marriage is the most important, most engrossing event with subject of endless conversation and is of most prolonged preparations with high esteem.

In some part of India marriage of a brother's children with the sister's children are allowed, but an aunt does not marry his nephew and marriage between the members of same 'Gotra' (same family / ancestor name) is tabooed and regarded as illegal. In arranged marriages; the age, qualification, beauty, physique, potency, wealth, family status, caste, 'gotra' and horoscope matching are considered for selection of suitable match of brides and bride grooms. Now a day arranged marriage, mutual agreed marriage, love marriage and inter-caste marriage are all getting accepted by the parents, families as well as the society and the rituals of the ceremony is also performed as usual.

Betrothal (Sagai): The preliminary part of the marriage ceremony is betrothal called as Sagai / Tilak / Nirbandh / Engagement Ceremony/ Ring ceremony at different parts of India. It takes place on an auspicious day before the marriage day. The bridegroom's parents with relatives reach the girl's house carrying with them flowers, fruits, sweets, new clothes / dress and presentation of a necklace or a ring for the girl. They ask girl's parents for the hand of the girl. A collective 'Puja' with oath is performed before local God or in local temple agreeing and accepting the marriage. Astrologers are then consulted for fixing the proper time for solemnizing the marriage.

Customs / Rituals: Customs and ceremonies of marriage are classified to three types namely, the caste custom, the family custom and the local customs and differ from region to region and even from village to village. The process has three successive stages, preliminary rituals, marriage ritual and succeeding / subsidiary rituals. These rituals are performed by worshipping Gods through the priests praying for boons and blessings for a happy union between husband and wife. Joining of hands, tying knot with each other's wedding outfits, Embracing and Exchange of garlands etc are the different type of customs prevailing in Indian society.

Mangal Kritya: One day before the marriage 'Mangal Kritya' is observed at both the houses of bride and bridegroom. Few ladies are invited to the house, are given new saris to wear, then they perform a Puja invoking God and family ancestors seeking blessing for the marriage. They establish a sacred pitcher placing a coconut over it with rice grains, flowers, vermilion, sandal paste, sacred grass etc and worship the same. A feast is served to friends, relatives and guests.

Dance & Music (Sangeet): Indian music of Shehnai and flute are regarded as auspicious for wedding ceremonies and is the heart and soul of Hindu / Sikh and Muslim marriages. On the day of 'Mangal Kritya', in the house of the bride, women usually sing songs and dance on the tune of the instruments. Young girls dance by playing popular marriage filmy songs and traditional marriage songs. The bride is also made to dance among them. In some cases, a week before the marriage ceremony, Ladies'-Sangeet (dance &music) takes place every day in the evening in both the bride and groom's house. In north-west India usually Giddha, Bhangra, Garba, Dandiya, Rouf, Chappeli, Thali Dance, Raasleela etc are performed as a very important part of the ritual.

Marriage Day: In the morning of the marriage day the bride and groom at their respective homes take the nuptial bath with turmeric paste and scented water. Friends, ladies from own family, close relatives, companions with their blessings and best wishes apply sacred turmeric paste on his/her body, pour bathing water to take this holy bath.

Own brother or cousin brother of the bride (would-be-brother-in-law of the groom) arrives the house of the groom with clothes, sweets, curd and sacred materials etc for inviting him to proceed to bride's place for marriage. A priest recites hymns and makes the groom's welcome-Puja by the would-be-brother-in-law to accept his invitation. The bridegroom, his relatives, friends and family members make preparations to proceed to the bride's house in procession.

Marriage Procession: The groom is decorated by cosmetics, sandal paste, scented perfumes, gorgeous dresses (Kurta and Pyjama) and attractive turban and crown on the head. A male child is also equally decorated and made to sit along with the groom. Both the groom and the child proceed to the bride's place sitting in a decorated car/ vehicle or riding on the back of a horse or carried by a gorgeous open decorated palanquin (as per their custom at different places). They are accompanied by a respectable procession of relatives and friends. The procession includes lighting arrangements, dancing ladies, dancing gents, musicians, music parties with drum beaters, trumpet and clarinet blowers, flute-players, shehnai-players etc. The dance and the music are performed with pomp and grandeur before entering the house of the bride. Various types of crackers with sparkling lights and sounds are ignited and displayed.

Greeting: After arrival of the groom at Bride's place, the father of the bride along with a priest come closer to the groom; welcome him by uttering sacred hymns by the priest. The groom and his party are given warm welcome by garlanding and spraying scented water, perfumes over them. They are accompanied by family members, relatives and friends of the bride to a well decorated sitting hall. In some places, 'Aarti' (waving burning lamp) of the groom is performed by ladies. Aarti is an antidote to evil influence of malevolence or jealous attitude / looks which may have been cast upon.

Garlanding (Jaimala): In some part of India the function of Jaimala (Garlanding) is prevalent. The bride along with companions arrives at the meeting place (the stage). The bride and groom exchange garlands. Exchanging garlands signifies their acceptance to each other as lifelong companions. The priest recites hymns for brining good fortune.

Wedding at Mandap: Ceremonies start when bride and groom are seated in the Mandap (Altar) in the company of their parents and the priest. Water is sprinkled to purify the Mandap. The priest recites over 24 names of lord Vishnu. The most sacred hymn, Gayatri-Mantra and salutations are offered to lords such as Ganesh, Vishnu & Lakshmi, Shiv & Parvati, Indra & Indrani, and deities of family, village and the place. The priest chants hymns from Vedas, worships with fresh flowers, coconut, rice, sugar, other grains, ghee, kumkum (saffron) etc. Incense, lights and camphor are burnt and waved before the God.

Honey & Yoghurt (Madhurparka): Father of the bride gives some honey and yoghurt to the Groom signifying sweetness and coolness in dealing with the bride. The priest recites the hymns by praying gods to arrive and grace the place with their all protecting presence along with their sweet pleasant atmosphere.

Gifting the bride (Kanyadaan): The bride stands facing the groom in the Mandap (Altar) holding betel leaves, betel nut, rice grains and a flower in her cupped hands. The priest touches their foreheads with the water pot. The bride's father holds her hands, offers her to the groom and asks to accept the responsibility of being her husband. The groom grasps the hand of the bride and accepts betel nuts etc from her, promises to protect and maintain the bride, will appreciate her merits and forgive her shortcomings. The relatives and guests bless them by wishing long, happy, healthy and fruitful life.

Wedding Knot: The wedding knot (end of bride's veil/scarf is tied to the end of the scarf on the groom's shoulder) is formed to signify the union of bride and groom. Prayers are uttered by the Priest wishing the union as firm as the famous legendary couples of (i) Indra & Indrani, (ii) Vibhavasu & Svaha (iii) Soma & Rohini, (iv) Nala & Damayanti, (v) Vaisravana & Bhadra, (vi) Vasistha & Arundati, (vii) Gauri & Shankara, (viii) Vishnu & Lakshmi. All of them are invoked here. After this, bride and groom sit around the sacred fire. Promises between the groom and bride are made for prosperity and happy married life.

Blessing Verses (Mangala Ashtaka): The groom is made to stand facing west direction. A cotton or silk cloth printed with symbol of 'Om' and 'Swastik' is held by two close relatives of the bride or the groom as a screen in front of the groom. The bride is guided by the maternal uncle and made to stand opposite the bride groom. Due to the screen, they do not see each other. The Priest chants eight verses of blessings from the epics (Purans) in praise of Lord Ganesh, the Brahman etc to bring good luck, health and prosperity to the couple. After this the screen is removed and the bride and groom garland each other and put few grains of rice on each other's head. Rice grains mixed with red 'KumKum' are distributed among the guests. The guests now put rice grains on the heads of the couple as their blessings.

Wish Fulfilling (Akshata Ropan): Bride and groom support each other with their wishes. The bride wishes to have good luck, happiness and prosperity in life. The groom says, 'I will help you in achieving them' and puts some rice grain on her head.

The groom also wishes to fulfil his obligations of becoming happy and prosperous. The bride puts some rice on his head and says, 'I will help you in achieving them'.

In some places, bride and groom fasten a yellow colour turmeric thread on each other's wrist symbolizing dutiful, fruitful, prosperous and affectionate marriage bond.

Vows before sacred fire, Agni (Panigrahan & Havan): The sacred fire (Agni) is lit and the couple takes their marriage vows with the fire (Agni) as the great witness. The groom takes in his right hand the bride's right hand and promises to be a good husband and prays that they live happily forever in life.

Some sacred wood (Banyan, Pippal, Mango etc.) and camphor is put into the sand altar / pulpit / container (Havan Kund) to ignite the fire. The priest offers oblation to the fire God and chants, "May you burn vigorously in order to increase your power. Similarly, may our children, our resources (cattle) and knowledge increases with your grace, May we be blessed with plenty of food and water". The bride sits on the right side of the bridegroom before the sacred fire facing the East. The priest chants hymns and asks the bride and groom to repeat those after him. Various prayers and requests are made to the sacred fire for their good luck and prosperity.

Moving around fire (Phere): Oblation is offered by the groom and the bride to the sacred fire for success in their marriage and for binding their relations. To strengthen her ties with her husband's family, the bride offers oblation to Agni, Varun and the Sun God. The bride and groom walk around the sacred fire seven times to take their seven wedding vows while the priest keep on reciting hymns offering mixture of herbs, clarified butter, rice grains to the sacred fire.

Seven steps (Saptapadi): Seven steps ceremony is essential for the completion of the marriage. The priest makes seven small heaps of rice in a line to the north of the sacred fire. The couple stands side by side.

The bride stands on the right side of the groom. The bridegroom puts his right hand on the bride's right shoulder and walks together. When the groom speaks the hymn, both take a step forward with their right foot and bring their left foot forward to stand still. Each step is taken with the right foot in a slow walk while hymn (Mantra) is recited. They take seven steps together and each step implies vows respectively for (i) Food and Livelihood (ii) Power and Strength (iii) Wealth and Prosperity (Iv) Happiness (v) Growth of Children (vi) Seasonal Pleasures (vii) Close Union, Life-long friendship, happiness and companionship. Now thereafter, the bride sits on the side closet to the groom's heart (left side).

Oblation (Ahuti): One more oblation made to the Fire God. The Priest offers the remaining gee / clarified butter to the Gods as one oblation. He sprinkles the holy water with a flower or grass blades in all four directions and also on the bride, groom and guests sitting in the 'Mandap'. The couple then stands and prays to Fire God and the Priest sprinkles the couple with holy water by a flower and blesses for riches, success, happiness, peace and prosperity. The bride's and groom's parents pray to god for long life and prosperity of the newlyweds. Now the marriage is completed.

Necklace of black beads (Mangal Sutra): The bridegroom ties a necklace of black beads on the bride's neck. This is a symbol of good fortune, love, affection and friendship for their whole life. The bride may give a gold chain or ring to the groom. The Mangalsutra is a sign of good luck and prosperity, and it should never be removed.

Vermilion (Sindur Dan): The wife seats on the left side of her husband, who fills the parting in the middle of her hair with vermilion (Sindur). Hymns are recited at this time referring to the wife as the symbol of all kinds of material prosperity and good luck to the groom's family.

Blessings by showering of flowers (Ashirwad by Pushpavarsha): Finally flowers and rice-grains are showered on the newlyweds by family, relations and friends. The couple then bows to their family elders and other elderly relations and guests for their blessings.

Thus the Hindu wife is not only a colleague or partner, but also an equal companion and a co-worker in all spheres of life. Any female in the house is considered to be Goddess of fortune (Lakshmi) and good luck.

Departure of bride (Vidai): Departure of bride and groom is a touching ceremony, in which the bride leaves her parents house to start living with her husband. All the companions, relatives, friends, parents and family members with tearful eyes express grief for the departure of their loving girl and bid her farewell with blessings and best wishes. Before leaving, the bride throws back three handfuls of rice and coin over her shoulders, towards her parental home. This is done to ensure wealth and prosperity remains in her home forever.

Welcome at Groom's House: On the arrival at the groom's house, the new couple is welcomed by the groom's mother, with a traditional Aarti. The bride is asked to knock a vessel filled with rice, kept at the entrance. She then dips her feet in a mixture of red vermillion and enters the house, leaving foot prints on the floor. This ritual is practiced as the bride is considered a form of Goddess Lakshmi. After this, a number of wedding games are played to make the bride comfortable. Furthermore, a reception party is organized by the groom's family in the evening. This is organized to welcome the new member and introduce her to the associates.

Chaturthi: On the 4th day of marriage the Chaturthi ceremony called as honeymoon is celebrated at Groom's place. A fire oblation with ceremonial worship by Priest takes place in the marriage stage (Mandap) where the bride and groom perform the rites as per the Priest's instruction. Where the oblation has not been performed on the marriage stage, the same is done at groom's place on this fourth day (Chaturthi day). This worship is offered to the ancestors to obtain their blessing for newlywed couple. Now a day, in addition to this function, the honeymoon is celebrated by the couple at a suitable tourist place for the sake of a memorable entertainment.

Ashtamangala: Up to 8th day from the marriage the adoration to the couple is made every evening by making them sit together on the marriage stage by wearing the sacred wedding dress, their aprons having wedding knot and wedding crowns on their head. These marriage uniforms are kept secured till 8th day. Elderly ladies of the house perform the adoration by waving lamp and worshipping them as the symbol of couple 'Laxmi Narayan'.

The bride feeds sweet / molasses to all the family members and relatives on 8th day in the house as a custom of faith to establish sweet relation with everyone. She offers obeisance to all the elder family members and take their blessings.

Chandra Vandapana: This function takes place on the second day of waxing phase of moon (Dwitiya Chand). The couple are made to sit on the marriage stage wearing new dresses with the wedding apron having knot. Moon worshipping by the couple takes place with chanting of hymns by the Priest. A small moon made of silver in the shape of second bright moon (Dwitiya Chand) comes from bride's house and is worshipped there. After the worship, the knot of couple's aprons is opened and taken out forever.

WELLNESS
BY OUR
WORSHIPS,
FESTIVALS & RITES

INVOCATION TO SUN GOD

(Shamba Dashmi)

In the month of **January,** on the 10th day of waxing phase of moon (Pausha Shukla Dashmi), the festival known as Shamba Dashmi is observed in east part of India. This religious observance has been mentioned in several epics / scriptures like Shamba Puran, Bhabishya Puran, Skandha Puran, Brahma Puran, Kapila Samhita and Mahabharat.

Shamba the son of Lord Srikrishna had suffered from the disease of 'Laprosy'. Famous monk 'Narada' advised him to arrive at a spot on eastern sea-coast of Bay of Bengal and worship the Sun-God. Shamba had performed the worship for 12 years at a place, the confluence of river Chandrabhaga with the ocean. He had discovered a statue of Sun-God in lotus posture. He built a sun-temple, established the statue inside the temple and continued worshipping there by taking holy dip in the river Chandrabhaga. From that day, worship of Sun-God could commence at the very place. In 9th Century, the world famous temple of **'Konark'** known as 'Black Pagoda' was built there by Odishan king 'Narsingh Dev' and the Sun-God used to be worshipped there. According to the name of Shamba it is called 'Shamba Dashmi'.

As per Brahma Puran, one Brahmin couple 'Gautam' and his wife 'Padma Mukhi' was in deep sorrow as their three sons died one after another and they became issueless. Gautam advised his wife Padmamukhi to worship Sun-God there. She followed his words and one day, the Sun-God came in to her vision and advised her to observe the sacred vow on this bright 10th day of month of 'Pausha' (Shukla Pausha Dashmi).

He further depicted her detail principles and methods of performing the worship for 3 times on this day.

Ladies keep a vow of religious observance and worship the Sun-God in early morning just after the sunrise by offering fruits. In the mid day at noon they again worship the Sun-God by offering rice-cakes (Pitha) and sweets. For the 3rd time at evening before the setting sun they worship again with offerings of cakes. The offered "Prasad" are distributed to assembled devotees and taken by the lady observing the religious vow as she keeps on fasting to that night. By celebrating this, it is believed that the family will have good luck; the issueless will be blessed with child and there won't be any unexpected disaster in the family.

Maharshi 'Narad' narrated this observance to the famous queen 'Rukmani' who followed the same and performed this sacred vow. Thereafter, Rukmani was blessed with her famous son 'Pradyumna', a talented and powerful prince. Pradyumna fought battle with a furious demon, 'Sambar' and defeated and killed him on that day. Therefore, the name of this day is also called as 'Sambar Dashmi'

Ladies of Odisha as stated above every year worship the Sun-God on this day in their house at open courtyard looking to the Sun 3 times in a day (at Sunrise, Noon and Sunset) with "Prasad"-offering of fruits, sweets and cakes. They keep this vow on the name of their son and daughter and while worshipping they sound / utter their names before the Sun-God for availing good luck.

Makar Sankranti

(Pongal)

First day of the month of 'Magha' is called Makar Sankranti and normally happens on **14th January** every year. Makar Sankranti is celebrated in India everywhere throughout the country. In South-India it is well known as Pongal and is celebrated with opulence for consecutive three days and in the state of Assam this is celebrated as 'Bihu'. In some of these states, their new year also begins on this day.

Sun travels from the tropic of Cancer (Karkat) to the tropic of Capricorn (Makar) by coming to the Makar Rasi (Zodiac) and proceeds towards the equator in its voyage towards north called **'Uttarain'**. Therefore it is called Makar Sankranti. It is believed that during the period of Uttaryan', if someone dies, he goes to heaven. From this day, duration of the day increases and that of the night decreases and winter cold gradually starts reducing. Even in foreign countries like Italy and Israel, the Romans and Jews celebrate this day as their festival.

On this day people perform funeral obsequies in honour of their ancestors. They perform special worships and oblation before Gods in temples. Raw rice, Molases, Cheese, Coconut, Sweet Potato, Sugarcane, Ghee, Honey, Banana, Milk are mixed and a unique "Prasad" is prepared as is called as 'Makar-grain'. The 'Revdi Sweet' made of Tils and Sugar is also prepared and offered to Gods. After offering to the God, **'Makar-grain'** as well as **'Revdi'** are taken by everybody and distributed to others. Devotees give charity to the poor; they give rice, lentil mixture (khichdi) and clothes as charity to the needy. Friends and colleagues establish bosom relationship among them by calling and becoming 'Makar' to each other. In villages, first two days are celebrated with vegetarian food and the 3rd day non-vegetarian food is taken with pleasure.

In Jagannath temple (Sri Mandir), it is a spectacular festival. 'Makar-grain' is prepared in big earthen vessels and taken to the temple premises. The Priests carrying this vessels walk around the temple in a procession with beating of drums and sounds of musical instruments. After completing 3 full rounds, the vessels are taken inside the temple and kept before the deities. Various cakes and curries and 24 types of Prasad are offered to the Gods with invocation and adoration.

Some places Lord Shiva and the Sun-God are worshipped on this day. In some places Godess Lakshmi with paddy, other grains, pulses, corns, agricultural equipments, cows, buffalos etc is worshipped. The house walls, floors and the entrance are decorated with handmade drawings using rice paste. In the tribal society this is a popular festival. They perform group dance and music with utmost pleasure and please their God by worshipping with dance and music.

A religious observation named as **'Dadhi Manthan'** (Stirring of Curd) is also celebrated on this day by cleaning, anointing the place of worship then marking 'Swastik' on the same, keeping rice grain and a vessel of curd on it. The curd is stirred by eulogizing and glorifying the song of Lord Krishna (Krishna Leela) from morning to noon. The importance of this day is mentioned in the famous 'Mahabharat' that Guru Dronacharya was issueless, but as per advice of Maharshi Durbasa, his wife solemnized 'Dadhi Manthan' on Makar Sankranti day in above manner with welcome of Sun-God and worshipping of Kid-Krishna with mother Yashoda. As a result, she was blessed with her heroic son Ashwathama. According to the epics, those ladies who observe 'Dadhi Manthan' on this day are gifted with handsome and talented son like Shri Krishna.

In different pilgrim places of the country, auspicious bathing-occasion happens on this day. In the religious city of Allahabad **(Prayag)** at Sangam, the famous Makar festival takes place. People in millions assemble there and take holy bath in the sacred river 'Ganges'.

In some part of the country (West and North) the kite flying festival is celebrated on this day. This day kite flying is considered as an integral part of celebrations all over India by young as well as old persons.

PONGAL: It is a harvest festival celebrated in Southern India especially in the state of Tamilnadu. In honour of the rain God, a 3 day long festival of thanks giving takes place. The Sun God is also worshipped along with the holy cow. The first day of the festival is known as **'Bogi Pongal'** and the rain God Lord Indra is worshipped this day. People clean their houses, paint and decorate them, burn junk or useless articles in a bonfire as preparations for the festival. Women make rangoli. People take bath, wear new clothes and pay obeisance to Lord Indra. They thank him for the rains that led to a good harvest and implore him to come again for the next harvest. Men and women dance around the bonfire and generally have a get-together. It is a community festival and is special for sisters who pray for the welfare of their brothers.

The second day of Pongal is dedicated to the Sun-God and is known as **'Surya Pongal'**. People express their thanks to him for giving heat and energy to the fields, which let to a bountiful yield of paddy crop. Fresh paddy is pounded to get new rise. Pongal dish is made in a new copper pitcher from new rice, jaggery, milk and butter. This rice dish is first offered to Lord Surya then it is distributed among all family members. People visit each other's house this day and sweets are exchanged.

The 3rd day of Pongal is for cattle and other animals. It is known as **'Mattu Pongal'**. People wash, clean and decorate their animals with bells, garlands and kumkum, and feed them with Pongal rice and bananas. A portion of this dish is also kept out in the open for the birds and insects. Then there is feasting and rejoicing. A favourite event is Bullfight **(Jallikatu)** which are organized in every town and village of the state. Villagers tie currency notes to the horns of the bulls and the young men try to snatch them from the horn. The successful men become local heroes.

BONFIRE

Festival of fire is an old tradition of India. In Veda, Epics and Scriptures creation of fire, its protection and related festivals have been described. Fire is one of the essential elements out of the 5 basic elements of creation such as Ether, Water, Fire, Wind and Earth. In North India, especially in the state of Punjab and Haryana, this is celebrated on 13th **January** evening as a seasonal harvest festival and called as **'Lohri'** which falls on the previous day of Makar Sankranti. In most places of Odisha, this festival also takes place at the same time and is called as festival of fire **(Agni Utsav)**. In some parts, this is performed on the morning of Makar Sankranti.

Lohri is a festival celebrated by the whole community in Punjab and Haryana with much fun and feasting. A huge bonfire is built by arranging a heap of dry fire woods in form of a pyramid and then is worshipped and lit. Sweets, sugarcane stalks, parched rice, fruits and sesame seeds etc are thrown in to the bon fire. People dressed in good clothes dance around the bonfire. Men do their foot-tapping **'Bhangra Dance'** to the beat of the 'Dholak' and women perform the **'Gidda Dance'**. People exchange revdi and other sweets, peanuts, popcorn and puffed rice. The fire has a practical aspect of warding off the cold air, which is prevalent at that time of the year.

New born baby's first Lohri is celebrated with much more gaiety and fanfare. Everybody is invited to join the party and dancing goes on till late night. It is auspicious for the farmers as they celebrate a good harvest and prepare for the next sowing season. Children like to fly kite on this day. Lohri is a fun filled festival of the fun loving people.

ODISHA'S BONFIRE (AGNI UTSAV): On full moon day of month of Magha (Magha Purnima) which falls normally on **middle of February,** the bonfire festival called as **'Agni Purnima'** is celebrated. It is said that in Vedic days monks, rishies used to perform sacrifice (Yajna) in the month of Magha and Falgun. Also to get rid of severe cold, attack from wild animals and to protect cornfields from harmful insects, flies and birds; this festival of bonfire has started. In the village, at evening of this day, people bring dry fire woods, straw of paddy and wheat etc from their house and assemble at a common place. A big bamboo is erected vertically on the soil. The fire woods are heaped surrounding the bamboo in the form of a huge pyramid. Village Brahmin (Pandit) worships the heap sounding hymns and offering Prasad. He accompanied with people travel around the bonfire for 7 times and then lights the bonfire.

Men and women move round the lighted bonfire with pleasure by collectively sounding God's name (Haribol) and with women's sacred joyous inarticulate sound (Hulahuli). They throw potato, brinjal, cabbage, tomato, banana and other vegetables to the fire. At the end after the full ignition, the pandit pacifies the fire by sprinkling sacred 'Panchamrit' which is prepared by mixture of milk, curd, ghee, honey and sugar. People search out the burnt vegetables from the ashes and collect it as "Prasad" of the Fire God. They take a portion of ash to their house and besmear on their forehead with holiness the next day this ash is sprinkled in the cornfield for better harvest. Next day morning village girls after taking bath go to the place of bonfire. They clean portion of the place and paint the place with drawings by rice paste. They worship the Sun-God by offering coconut, banana, raw rice, milk and ghee to the Sun-God. In present day trend this ceremony is a people's festival.

It is believed that on this day the elephant while crossing the river was attacked by a crocodile-bite and therefore, he prayed the Lord God for rescue. God had saved him by killing the crocodile. Therefore, Lord Jagannath is dressed on this day with the appearance of **'Elephant-Saviour'.** Thousands of people visit the temple on this day to have a holy glance of the Lord.

BASANT PANCHAMI

Saraswati Puja

asant Panchami falls on bright 5th day of the month of Magha which normally happens in **1st week of February**. Goddess Saraswati who bestows the gift of education, music, dance and the arts on people is worshiped on this day. In eastern India Saraswati Puja is a revered festival. On this day, books, pen, pencil, musical instruments and paint brushes are worshipped and kept near the idol of Goddess Saraswati to seek her blessings. In educational institutions students perform the worship with pomp and many cultural events are organized. It is considered as an auspicious day to begin any new course of study or arts.

In early morning students collect flowers from the locality and make garlands. After taking bath they wear new clothes carry the garlands to the school where they decorate the place of worship. Clay statue of Goddess Saraswti is installed on a stage. The statue is decorated with sari, flowers and garlands. The Pandit (Priest) is invited to perform Puja. All of them sit down on the floor for worshipping the goddess. After a long process of puja ceremony, fire oblation takes place. They pray the Goddess seeking study, knowledge, arts and literature etc. At the end, as per the direction of the Priest, they offer handful of flower (Puspanjali) to the Goddess 3 times with mass-praying by folded palms and uttering hymn.

In Odisha and Bengal, worship of Goddess Saraswati is very ancient. From 9th century Goddess Saraswati is found carved on the temple body.

Famous poet late 'Sarala Das' and other reputed writers, poets have expressed that Goddess **'Sarala'** is Devi Saraswati, the embodiment of learning and arts. According to the poet Sarala Das Goddess Sarala is the ancient mother as Mahalakshmi, Mahasaraswati, Durga and benefactor of education, wisdom and learning.

Teachers, students, writers, poets, and musicians they do visit Goddess Sarala on this day to get her blessings. Dramatists, artists of Opera and musicians present their first public performance outside the entrance of Sarala temple premises.

Thus, 'Basant Panchmi' ushers in the spring season music, dance and frolic.

In the temple of Shri Jagannath, 'Basant festival' is celebrated with pomp and splendour.

MAHA SHIVRATRI

Maha Shivratri festival or the Night of Lord Shiva is celebrated with devotion and religious fervour. This falls on the moonless 14th night of the new moon in the month of Phalgun, corresponding to English month **February**. This marks the wedding day of Lord Shiva and Parvati. Some believe that lord Shiva performs the 'Tandava' dance of the creation, preservation and destruction on this auspicious night.

Worship of Lord Shiva continues all through the day and night. Every 3 hours priests perform ritual puja of Shivalingam by bathing it with milk, yoghurt, honey, ghee, sugar and water amidst the chanting of 'Om Namah Shivay' and ringing of temple bells. The temple reverberates with the sound of bells and words of praise for Lord Shiva.

Devotees observed strict fast in honour of lord Shiva. Many go on a diet of fruits and milk; some do not consume even a drop of water. Devotees strongly believe sincere worship of lord shiva on this auspicious day of Shivratri absolves a person of sins and liberates him from the cycle of birth and death. The devotee reaches the aboard of lord Shiva and lives there happily being liberated from worldly life and attains salvation (moksha). It is considered especially auspicious for women. Married women pray for the well being of their husbands, unmarried women pray for an ideal husband, like Lord Shiva.

Devotees circumambulate the 'Linga', three or seven times, and then pour water, milk, bilva-leaves, flower, honey, butter, ghee, rosewater and other gifts over it. Worship of lord Shiva consists night long vigil (jagran) is observed in Shiva temples where large number of devotees spend the night, singing hymns and devotional songs in praise of Lord Shiva. Only in the following morning the devotees break their fast by partaking "Prasad" offered to the Deity.

According to the Shiva Puran, the Maha Shivratri worship must incorporate six items:

- Bathing the 'Shiva-Linga' with water, milk and honey and wood apple or bel leaves added to it, representing purification of the soul.
- The vermilion paste applied on the 'Shiva-Linga' after bathing, represents virtue;
- Offering of fruits, which is conducive to longevity and gratification of desires;
- Burning incense, yields wealth;
- The lighting of the lamp which is conducive to the attainment of knowledge;
- And betel leaves marking satisfaction with worldly pleasures

'Tripundra' refers to the three horizontal stripes of holy ash applied to the forehead by worshippers of Lord Shiva. These stripes symbolise spiritual knowledge, purity and penance (spiritual practice of Yoga), so also they represent the three eyes of Lord Shiva.

Wearing a rosary made from the Rudraksha-seed of the Rudraksha tree (said to have sprung from the tears of Lord Shiva) when worshipping Lord Shiva is ideal.

FESTIVAL OF COLOURS

(Holi)

This is a festival of hues and colours welcoming the advent of pleasant colourful bright spring season. It is celebrated in the month of 'Phalgun' on the full-moon day (mid-**March**). At some places it is celebrated on the next day of full moon and some places on both these days. It is observed with great pomp; show, fun and frolic and brings joy and merriment everywhere. It is harbinger of flowers and roses and is a festival of joy.

People bid good bye to the chilly winter, welcome the change of season, put on colourful dresses. People of all cast, colour and creed forget their differences, old amnesties; assemble in their community-places, clubs, roads, markets, courtyards and houses to sprinkle on them the colour called 'Gulal', 'Abeer', smear all sorts of colours, spray coloured waters on everybody, embrace each other and exchange best wishes. It results in communal harmony and brotherhood.

Children enjoy the most; they play with water colours and balloons. They leave shyness, become bold and do not even spare a stranger or passer-by. Their innocent joy and play with colours are taken as harmless and funny.

People visit their friends and relatives. They first smear dry colours on their foreheads; sprinkle coloured water and hug each other. They renew their friendship and bond of relationship. Any misunderstanding earlier gets washed out in colours. People prepare sweets, namkeens, savouries and offer to each other. Gujias, Thandai, Pakoda, Dryfruits and sweets are remarkable snacks offered, served and exchanged. Serving, sharing snacks along with spray of colour, wishing and embracing each other are great pleasant and memorable events of Holi.

In the famous place of Mathura and Vrindavan, it is believed that Lord Krishna used to play Holi with the 'Gopis' on this day in 'Dwapar Yug'. Even today the Holi celebration at these places is grand and unique.

On the previous evening of Holi, the bonfire is worshipped. Dry woods are kept in a heap are ignited by fire. After the fire is lit, people go around the fire offer "Prasad", fruits and green grams etc to the fire. All pray the Fire-God for goodness of the society, good harvest that year. They anoint the ashes of fire on their forehead with the belief of good health and good days ahead.

According to the legend, the demon king 'Hiranyakashyapu' wanted to kill his son, 'Prahlad' as he was a devotee of Lord Vishnu and refused to acknowledge his father as supreme god. The king arranged to make his sister 'Holika' to sit down on the bonfire taking 'Prahlad' in her lap. Knowing the fact that Holika could not be harmed by the fire due to a boon from god and 'Prahlad' would die; it was lit by fire. But by the grace of Lord Vishnu, 'Prahlad' emerged unscathed from fire and Holika was burnt to ashes. Later Lord Vishnu took the incarnation as 'Narsimgha' and killed 'Hiranyakashyapu'. Therefore, the fire is symbolic of destruction of all evils and the festival is called as festival of 'Holi'.

As per another legend, on this day, lady demon 'Putna' tried to kill infant Lord Krishna but she failed and; Krishna killed Putna by sucking all milk from her. Further, on this day the love-god 'Kamadev' was destroyed by Lord Shiva's anger as Kamadev has tried to break meditation of Lord Shiva. Ultimately by the prayer of Kamadev's consort 'Rati'; Lord Shiva relented and gave back his life.

Swinging Festival (Dola): From 10th day of waxing phase of moon (Shukla) upto this Holi fullmoon—day of the month of Phalgun; for five days this festival of 'Swinging God' known as Swinging Festival (Dola) is celebrated. It is called Dola Purnima or Dola Yatra or Vasant Utsav. The main god for this festival is 'Lord Krishna and goddess Radha'. Their moving idols are placed in a cradle situated inside a celestial car or chariot called Viman and is taken around the village from house to house. The Viman is lifted manually by group of people and kept on their shoulders and carried along the village road to each house. The house owner worships the gods through the accompanying priest, presents "Prasad" and offers some dues to the priest.

On the full moon day the idols of Radha Krishna are taken from the temple to the "Swinging-Altar" (platform) known as 'Dola Bedi' where their special worship is performed. Fire oblation is offered with chanting of Vedic hymn.

In Shri Mandir of Lord Jagannath at Puri, this function is very auspicious and is performed with grandeur in presence of thousands of devotees. The new Almanac (Panjika) having forecast of the New Year is inaugurated before the god at this altar.

Dola Fair: Ultimately at evening on this Holi day, all the Vimans with moving idol of Lord Krishna and Radha of surrounding villages and temples are carried to an open field, the place of rendezvous which is called as 'meeting ground' of gods or the field of festival / fair (Dol Yatra). The Vimans are placed in a circle producing a panoramic view. Crackers are fired and displayed in air. In front of the gods, local artists perform dancing, singing devotional songs, chorus etc. Smearing of Gulal (Fagu), Abeer takes place. "Prasad" with especially new mango buds are offered. The ground gets crowded by thousands of people from nearby villages. Many shops, stalls and traders display their goods for sale. Restaurants, juice corners, syrups, soft drink shops, local foods and eatables are sold there. Rural people take part in the festival offering obeisance to gods; enjoy the music, dance, shopping and delicious foods.

Ritual of killing sheep-demon: The Vimans are carried back to their permanent place of worships in temples. Before entering to their altar / pulpit in the temple, a small ritual is performed. A small hut made of straw made near to the temple is lit by fire to burn. The god is taken around the fire seven times and then is taken in to the temple to his permanent altar. This event memorizes the killing of a notorious 'sheep-shaped demon' by lord Krishna in Vrindavan and burning the demon's hut by the public.

NAV RATRA & RAM NAVAMI

Lord Rama is seventh incarnation of Lord Vishnu in Tretaya Yug. Ram Navami is the birth day celebration of Lord Rama. It falls on 9th day of waxing phase of moon (shukla paksha). In the month of Chaitra (**March-April**) Ram Navami is observed by Hindus throughout India. The eight days preceding Ram Navami are celebrated as **Navratra** in northern India. In other words, Ram Navami marks the end of the auspicious **Navratra** period, when goddess 'Durga' is worshipped.

In this festival, devotees observe a fast, worship lord Rama and sing devotional songs. At Ayodhya, the birthplace of Rama, it is celebrated with special joy. Tableau depicting the life of Rama is put up in the festooned temples. Discussions on the famous epic Ramayana takes place everywhere. Lord Rama was embodiment of incomparable power, heroism, truthfulness, honesty, benevolence and of idealistic character. Ram Rajya is his exemplary kingdom existed during his tenure. Therefore, all time in the history; people, kings and rulers, endeavour to establish such administration, such a kingdom called Ram Rajya.

People keep a religious observance on this day. They clean their house; arrange flower, fruit, sacred doob-grass, ghee, incense, earthen lamp, oblation materials etc. They worship Lord Rama, Lakshman, Sita, and Hanuman with these materials. With utmost devotion, they meditate, pray the Lord, chanting hymns, offering flowers and holy basil leaves. At various public places; opera, drama, dance, chorus, music, eulogy on life history of Rama (Ramleela) are performed for several days commencing from Ram Navami.

In Jagannath temple at Puri, Ram Navami festival is celebrated with pomp and grandeur. Lord Jagannath is one incarnation of Lord Shri Ram, therefore lord Jagannath is decorated as Shri Ram and his birth day is observed on this day in the temple, 'Sri Mandir'.

EASTER & GOOD FRIDAY

Easter, is the most sacred Christian festival and a holiday. It is celebrated on the first Sunday after the full moon following March Equinox and varies between 26th March and 25th April. It is the resurrection of Jesus Christ on the 3rd day after his crucifixion and a day of great joy for the followers of Christianity. **Good Friday** is the day on which Jesus was crucified and **Easter** day is the day on which Jesus came back to life. **"Passover"** commemorates the time when God rescued people of Israel from slavery and led them out of Egypt. Jesus, a Jew, was crucified during Passover time. It is Jesus crucifixion and resurrection that led to the start of Christianity. Both Easter and Passover revolve around the idea of rebirth. Jesus was resurrected or born again and the slaves were reborn into freedom.

Easter Custom varies across the Christian world, by attending sunrise services with greeting, clipping the church and decorating Easter Eggs. Easter marks the end of the forty-day period of **Lent**, which starts in February or March, from Wednesday. It is said that from this day Lord Jesus Christ fasted in the desert and began to preach. This forty-day period is for purification and penance, and the last week is known as the **Holy Week**. This week is reserved for austerity, meditation, and prayers. The Sunday before Easter is known as **Palm Sunday** after the time when Lord Jesus entered Jerusalem and was greeted by waving of palm fronds. The day of the Last Supper is known as **Maundy Thursday**, when he instituted the Eucharist or communion service in which bread is broken and shared.

Good Friday, the day of Lord Christ's crucifixion is the day for mourning, sermons, prayers and fast. People go to the Church for the ceremony. It is believed that since Lord Christ died for the good of mankind, this day is particularly holy, hence the name Good Friday. Many churches celebrate Good Friday with a subdued service, usually in the evening, in which Christ's death is remembered with solemn hymns, prayers of thanksgiving, a message centered on Christ suffering for our sakes, and observance of the Lord's Supper.

On **Easter Sunday** Christians believe Jesus Christ was resurrected from the dead and God's kingdom of love and forgiveness was established. Therefore, Christians exchange good wishes amongst themselves on this day.

FIRST BAISAKH

(Baisakhi)

First day of the month of Baisakh is called "Baisakh Sankranti" or "Mesh Sankranti" or "Bishuba Sankranti" or "Pana Sankranti" or "Shakkar Pongal" in India. It occurs usually in **Mid April**. On this day Sun remains on the equador (Bishuba), therefore the duration of day and night become equal.

It is an auspicious day. In the war field of Mahabharat; while the grand old father Bhisma was lying on bed of arrows, he felt very much thirsty. He requested Arjuna to feed him water. There was no water near to the war field. Arjuna being helpless had shot an arrow to the earth in search of water. A stream of water came out. Bhisma could drink this water and was extremely satisfied. Before his breathing last, he had said, "on this day those who will feed water to thirsty people, they will be free from all diseases and miseries. They will lead happy life by receiving the blessings of Gods and ancestors." From that day, the tradition of offering water to the thirsty is continuing in our society. People provide water at different places, on the road side and invite the travellers to halt for a while and to drink water, buttermilk, soft drinks, curd water etc and proceed. Starting from this day, this service continues for a month to mitigate the sufferings from the scorching summer heat of the Sun.

In villages, people water the trees; especially they water daily the roots of the holy Basil plant, Banyan tree and Pipul Tree. They pour water over the statues of Gods and Goddesses. A pitcher having a tiny hole in the bottom is kept hanging over the God. A sacred piece of "Doob grass" is inserted into the hole, so that, continuous droplets of water flows in controlled manner and falls upon the head of the Deity. People visiting the Deity carry water, pour into the pitcher and worship the God. It is called "Basudhara". The aim of the system is to protect the earth from heat of sunrays.

This day, people prepare in their house foods out of grams, peas, cicer, arietinuum, parched rice, wheat-corn powder, Bel fruit (aegle marmelos) curd, cheese, soft drinks to feed visitors, Brahmins, poor people arriving at their house. According to their own status and capabilities; they offer various gifts to such visitors. These people arrive in houses in groups throughout the day. Rich people after serving food, offer money, new clothes, shoes, wooden sandals, slippers (chappal), umbrella, towels, pens, pencils, notebooks appropriately to them. All of them express their good will, blessings and appreciation to the house holder's family. Especially the Brahmins, one by one bless all family members by touching their heads.

Patua Yatra (Fair): Many people perform ceremonial functions, sacrifice, god-worships, oblation etc on this auspicious day. It is believed that Gods and Goddesses have descended from heaven to earth on this day; therefore worshipping Gods on this day saves us from misfortunes. In villages of eastern India, this day is celebrated as closing ceremony of a fair called "Patua Yatra" which are of different kinds such as 'Jhamu', 'Patua', 'Danda' and 'Uda' etc. These yatra or fairs are celebrated in renowned Goddess-temples and also in temples of Lord Shiva and continue for one month.

Patua Dance: The Patua-dancer comes to village and performs in front of houses. Throughout the month, the "Patua" and his associates, beating their gongs, walk down in village streets and visit house to house. The arrival of the "Patua" is acknowledged by hearing the sounding of gong from a distance. "Patua" is a male devotee of the nearby famous Goddess. One such Goddess "Sarala" in the state of Odisha has such famous "Patua" display. Her "Patua" visits houses in villages carrying a pitcher on his head. His body with head and face are well dressed as like a Goddess. He wears a black coloured 'Ghaghda' with a red coloured blouse and two pieces of upper garments (cloths) which hang down from his left and right side originating from the head-pitcher. The pitcher is of special shape, decorated with pastes of vermilion, sandal wood, turmeric and flower garlands. The pitcher is filled with sacred bathing turmeric water of the famous Goddess "Sarala" carried from the temple.

The Patua having dressed in such dress and carrying the decorated holy pitcher on the head represents the mother Goddess "Sarala". He releases hands leaving the pitcher free on his head. Then he holds left hanging garment by left hand and night hanging garment by right hand and starts dancing by keeping balance of the head with the pitcher. He shows different postures by bending, rotating and sitting. Keeping the pitcher freely on head without supporting by hand and then performing dance is a skilful art. During his dance, his associates beat the gongs and sing spiritual songs. People pay homage to the Goddess. At the end, the Patua applies vermilion on foreheads of all the audience by taking it from outside body of the pitcher. He worships the pitcher-goddess on behalf of the house owner by uttering some sacred words. All family members offer prayer with obeisance. Patua lifts the pitcher and tilts it on everyone's head. The holy water droplets fall on them. Finally the Patua is given cash reward by the house owner and he leaves happily. Thus the moving goddess travels from village to village and arrives at the doorstep of the devotees giving a holy vision.

Ecstatic Patua: There are various kinds of "Patua". They observe fasting on this day and assemble at riverside or at a pond to the evening. As per their custom, they take bath and worship the Goddess there. One of them preferably, a woman feels that the Goddess has appeared inside her body. She displays extraordinary energy, abnormal behaviour, vigorous body movements, ecstatic dance, and talks violently by spinning her head with open hairs; holding a cane in one hand and holding a pot of burning resins in the other hand. All devotees assembling there worship her; pray her by waving lamps offering fruits, food and flowers. After some time she slows down, becomes normal and recovers. After her recovery, all take food and return home.

Jhamu Yatra: Other Patuas celebrate "Jhamu Yatra". In this yatra; devoted Patuas observe fasting, worship the Goddess and happily take different physical pains showing their tricks and skills as mentioned below.

"Foda Patua" is one kind of Patua who pierce nails into their body at both sides of waist, tie spoons to the nails. After filling burning resins in these spoons they perform dancing.

"Kanta Patua" walks barefoot over a bed of nails.

"Nian Patua" walks barefoot over hot bed of burning fire.

"Khanda Patua" walks barefoot on sharp edge of two swords (daggers).

"Pani Patua" shows gymnastics in water of a river or pond or a lake.

"Jhada Patua" climbs a date-tree by barefoot against the sharp edges and break number of branches remaining on the tree.

"Uda Patua" ties himself to a bamboo-pole attached to a pillar. Then he rotates runs and flies several times around the pole.

Dand Yatra: "Dand Yatra" or "Dand Dance" has started from worshipping of Lord Shiva. It is performed for 21 days starting from Purnima (full moon day) and ends on this Bishuba Sankranti day. Thirteen nos. of devotees participate in this. A water filled pitcher known as "Kamna Ghat" (desire-pot) is worshipped. A bamboo pole with 13 knots is tied with a piece of cloth at the tip and is kept in a house named as "Kamna Ghar" (desire-house). This pole is called as "Dand" representing Lord Shiva and is worshipped there. Devoted artists in this 'Dand-Yatra' demonstrate different kinds of exercises, yoga and some tricks.

Dand Nat: Drama / Play are staged on popular stories from epics and is depicted by acting with poetic expressions. Musical instruments like drum, gong, conch, trumpet and cymbal are played. In the play called

"Dand-Nat", the acting groups put on different dresses and appear in different forms like (i) Shiva-Parvati, (ii) Hunter-man & woman, (iii) Saura-man & woman, (iv) Bird-man & woman, (v) Gipsy-man & woman, (vi) Jambab, (vii) Kalika, (viii) Yogi etc and perform stage show to amuse the audience. They also move round on streets and villages performing their arts from door to door.

"Patua Yatra", "Jhamu Yatra" and "Dand Yatra" are very significant in the social and cultural life of Odisha.

Bihu Festival

'Bihu' festival is most popular festival of Assam. It is combination of three Bihu festivals—'Rangoli Bihu (Bohang)' celebrated in spring (**mid-April**), 'Prasadali Bihu' in winter (**mid-January**) and 'Kati Bihu' in Autumn (**mid-October**).

Rangoli Bihu (Bohang): This is the celebration of sowing season. People wear new colourful clothes, visit their neighbours, friends, relatives distribute sweet and greet each other a Happy Bihu. Colourful rituals mark the first day of Rangoli Bihu and is called 'Gori Bihu' which is dedicated to cattle and live stock. Household cattle are given guest treatments, wear flower garlands and are fed with good food. Rest of the week long celebrations of 'Rangoli Bihu (Bohang)' are known as 'Manuh Bihu'. A mood of festivity and gaiety is observed throughout Assam during these seven days of celebration. On the 7th day of festival, seven types of leafy vegetables are prepared. The next day is called as 'Gosain Bihu' which is observed with several religious traditions.

Rangoli Bihu derives its name from the Sanskrit word 'Vishuvam' meaning vernal equinox when day and night is of equal duration. People welcome spring season and pray for a bountiful and rich harvest. 'Bohary' is name of 1st month of the Assamese calendar, corresponding to mid-April, normally comes on 13th April. Traditional festive food is the 'Pitha', a special rice-cake. The celebration is joyous, colourful and vibrant. Marking the occasion, young boys and girls in village dress-up traditional cloth; men wear 'Dhoti', 'Kurta', tie Gamosa (towel) around their head and waist. Ladies wear Saadar Mekhala with a red blouse and they sing folk Bihu songs (Bihugeet) in traditional bihutolis or Mukoli

Bihus. The accompanied orchestra of Dhol (Drum), Pipa (buffalo hornpipe) and Gagana add joys to the celebrations.

At several places, Bihu fairs are also organised where people participate in the games and other fun filled activities. Bihu dance and Bihu songs are an integral part of Bihu festival. Bihu dance is synonymous to Assam and is a dance of joy. Both men and women perform the dance with great enthusiasm which reflects in their facial expressions and body movements. Dance variations are seen in dance among different tribes. The dance is coupled with Bihu songs which reflect the folk poetry touching the themes like love, daily life and New Year. Open fields, groves and stages become the venue for the joyous dance. The dance truly picturises a feast for eyes.

The 'Prasadali Bihu' celebrated in mid-January is a harvest festival marking the end of harvesting season. This festival is dedicated to feasts. Different kinds of Pithas (rice cakes) are prepared on this day. People offer prayer to 'God of Fire' in this festival.

'Kati Bihu', in mid-October the 3rd festival is one day long celebration prior to the harvesting season. Tulsi is worshipped in this festival.

MAHAVIR JAYANTI

The most important Jain festival, **Mahavir Jayanti** is celebrated on the thirteenth day of the Chaitra month of rising moon to commemorate the birthday of Lord Mahavir who was a saint and founder of **Jain** religion. It is a peaceful religion that cherishes simplicity. Their core values are such that they do not believe in killing even an insect. The mood of this festival is just a quiet celebration with respect to their saint. Worshiping rituals are not very elaborate or striking as Lord Mahavir was against idol worship in its ideal sense.

Mahavir Jain was born in the 5th century B.C. in a palace of Vaishali (in Bihar) to king Siddhartha and queen Trisala. After running his kingdom faithfully till 30 years of his age, the great saint gave up all luxuries and comforts of palace, remained in penance for twelve long years and was enlightened. He gave up all redundancies of life, would eat on his palms refusing to use a plate, and gave up wearing clothes. Getting rid of these rudimentary materials he focused on the real things and the real meaning of life. He preached the importance of truth and non-violence along with the message of not owning anything and not stealing. He had vowed to utilize his knowledge for the welfare of the masses and the upliftment of the underprivileged. He had taught '**Three Ratnas**' namely Right Conduct, Right Knowledge and Right Faith. He formulated his teachings into the famous religion **Jainism.**

The festival is celebrated throughout the country among Jain communities. Although they believe in simplicity and avoid grandiosity, there are some significant ceremonies that they uphold. One of the most significant traditions of this day is the visit to various Tirthankar statues and temples. There are processions with pictures and images of Mahavir.

The temples have varied worshipping to honour the statue of Mahavir by flowers, rice, fruits and consecrate (abhishek) it with milk. There are places of gathering or temples where the core values and message of Mahavir is preached. At some places, his life history is also told. Some of the believers observe a fast on this day. Kheer (frumenty) is prepared in most houses as a sweet dish.

Lord Mahavir, as it is believed in Jainism was born somewhere around the 5th century B.C. His birth date is on the thirteenth day of 'Chaitra' month of rising moon and falls in the month of April. The most important places of celebration of Mahavir Jayanti are Gujarat and Rajasthan. Gujarat is said to have to maximum number of Jain shrines. They are also the states where highest numbers of Jains reside. In India, Gujarat holds the biggest fair for this festival. Palitana and Girnar are some of the most significant places of worship of the state. Yet Vaishali, in Bihar, being the birth place of Mahavir, has its own importance and also celebrates this Jayanti significantly.

DEVOTIONAL HORSE DANCE

This is about worship of the goddess "Baseli". Mainly the fishermen celebrate this festival with grandeur and they take it to every home performing the famous folk dance of Odisha and Eastern India called 'Ghoda Nach' (Horse-Dance). This festival starts from Chaitra Purnima (**mid April**) upto Baisakh Purnima (middle of May). Goddess Baseli the tutelary goddess of the dynasty of fisherman is worshipped with pomp in the whole month. It is said that as per the wishes of Lord Bishnu, the horse faced goddess Baseli was born and was offered to the fisherman king. Since then the celebration is continuing by fisherman till now.

This dance was prevalent in all villages of east-coast Odisha in past. Now, this folk dance is available in remote villages. This dance is sometimes seen in Odia national TV (Doordarshan) as a folk dance. In the morning of any particular day of this month of April; village fisherman presents a big fresh fish at the houses of affluent villagers as token of invitation to watch his horse-dance which he would bring to night to perform at their front courtyard. House-owner then prepares to arrange articles for the worship of goddess Baseli, purchases new sari, new clothes, sweets, and keeps cash for giving them reward after performance of Horse dance before his courtyard.

As per tradition, on the **full moon day of the month of 'Chaitra' (April),** worship of goddess 'Baseli' along with horse-dance is performed. A long piece of bamboo is worshipped on this day. After that the same bamboo is torn longitudinally and converted to few pieces. These pieces are taken to make the shape (frame) of a horse. The frame is then covered by a coloured cloth. One horse face is made out of wood. This wooden horse face after getting painted is fitted into the neck of the horse body.

Thus it is a man-made horse carrier and is called as "Chaiti Ghoda" (Chaiti Horse). Two nos such framed horse are prepared. A garland of china-rose flower is put on the neck of the horse. These newly built horses are worshipped for 7 continuous days. On 8th day, this horse is taken outside to perform horse dance.

After mid night, the group of horse-dance arrive at village houses sounding their music of drum and trumpets. All members of the family and neighbours, they get up by their musical sound and assemble to witness the dance. Worshipping the goddess is done first. Two framed horse-carriers with male riders, one for each becomes ready for dancing.

The riders enter into the stomach, the middle cavity portion of framed horse. They lift the carrier (frame) keeping it supported over their shoulders and protruding their head outside. Musical instruments, Drums, Trumpets are played in a rhythm, known as music of horse-dance. These two persons protruding head and carrying each horse frame on shoulders perform horse-dance by emulating the musical measures. Other members of the dance group sing the devotional song meant for the goddess. At the same time, a couple dance dressed in male & female is performed. It is the dance of fisherman and woman with melodious songs accompanied by musical instruments. The lyric, tune, music and the rhythm of horse dance are unique and specific. The atmosphere becomes pleasant, attractive and full of emotions.

At the end; the affluent house owner presents sari, clothes, gift-money as reward. Others also offer money according to their wish. The troupe of horse dance then moves out to another house of the village for performance.

IMPERISHABLE DAY

(Akshaya Tritiya)

I n the month of Baisakh on the 3rd day of lunar fortnight, (beginning of **May**) this is an auspicious day called as "Akshaya Tritiya" (the Imperishable Day) Akshaya means imperishable. On this day all good works are initiated, It is believed that whatever noble work done on this day, yields good result and remains forever as imperishable. That is why; people start their various activities on this day.

Hindus believe in astronomical cycle of four ages of the world such as Satya Yug (Golden age), Treta Yug (Lord Ram's time), Dwapar Yug (Lord Krishna's time) and Kali Yug (Iron Age). It is said that the Golden age which is supreme for truth and happiness was initiated on this day. In every house of eastern India specially in Odisha, this day is celebrated as a festival. This festival is relating to cultivation. All farmers start sowing paddy seeds on this day.

This day, land owner and his helpers, servants get up early morning to prepare for the occasion. After taking holy bath in village pond, they wear new cloths. The seeds of paddy are collected from their stored earthen pots or straw boxes or stored gunny bags. A new paddy-measuring pot called "Gauni" is brought. A small branch of mango tree, some raw rice, turmeric, sandal, vermilion, beetle-nut, doob-grass, some "Prasad", some manures; all these are kept inside the "Gauni". After carrying these, they proceeded to the paddy field. In the paddy field, the land owner / farmer worships the goddess Laxmi (Fortune Goddess) at the north-east (Ishan) corner of the field praying for good yield. After this, the sowing of paddy seeds is inaugurated by his own hand. Then the helpers take over and continue sowing seeds in the paddy field. As per tradition, vegetarian food is served in the house on this day.

India is a country with agricultural base. Cultivation is their prime profession. Hence irrespective of cast and religion, farmers of eastern India religiously celebrate this day like the above manner. According to epic, goddess "Ganga" on this day descended from heaven to earth in form of a river. Ganga is the goddess of water. Goddess of grain and Goddess of water are equally important as both have originated from one goddess "Durga". Therefore on this day, to commemorate them, activity of sowing seed is commenced.

On this imperishable day all good works like sacred thread ceremony, marriage, inauguration of new house, sacrifices, contributions of food etc are performed. Feeding water to thirsty on this day is taken as a religious and important duty. Married women worship goddess "Shathi" praying for well being of their family.

In the most significant event of famous Car Festival of Lord Jagannath, the construction of the three giant chariots (Cars) begins from this day. The day is so auspicious that this age-old tradition continues every year from time immemorial. Prior to this day, long heavy wooden logs are brought and kept on the grand wide road at Puri town called as 'Grand Road' (Bada-Dand) of Lord Jagannath. The skilled group of carpenters on this day assemble there and perform adoration ceremony of praying the Lord for having success in constructing the Chariots. After this, they start making the Chariots.

Jaydev, the great poet and devotee of Lord Jagannath was born on this day. He has written the devotional song, famous "Geetgovind" in Sanskrit as a symbol of his ardent devotion to Lord Jagannath which is a pride and honour to the Hindus.

May Fair: The grand festival of water voyage called **"Chandan Yatra"** **(May-Fair)** of Lord Jagannath begins from this auspicious day to cool down the gods. It continues for 21 days. As the hot summer days of

May is unbearable, so applying the paste of sandalwood as coolant, waving wind by hand fans, waving chamer (Chowrie), blowing cold air and serving cold items to the Lord are followed. At evening, the famous water voyage starts with performance of dance, music, devotional songs, and opera. The Gods are ferried in decorated water boat by several times rotating and swirling on water. Throughout the night the fair continues. This festival at Puri is extremely enjoyable and pleasant.

On account of all the above remarkable events and ceremonies; this "Imperishable Day" is memorable and sacred.

BUDDHA PURNIMA

In the month of Baisakh, (May) the full moon day is known as Buddha Purnima, the most festive day for Buddhist. Gautam Buddha was born on this day in 526 B.C. and attained **Nirvana** or enlightenment on this day. Buddha found his moksha and died on this very day. To commemorate Lord Buddha's three major events, birth, enlightenment and demise; this day is celebrated.

Gautam Buddha was born as Prince Siddhartha at **Lumbini** of Rupandehi district. Siddhartha got married to Yashodhara and they had a son named Rahul. One day, Prince Siddhartha went around the city in his chariot, driven by his old faithful servant. There he met four sights which changed his entire life. He saw an old man, a sick man, a dead man, and an ascetic. The servant told him that everybody on this earth has to pass through the first three stages in their lifespan.

This made Siddhartha pensive and he began to question the purpose of the very existence of human beings, if they have to die one day. One night, Prince Siddhartha left his home in search of truth. On the full moon day of Baisakh, he found the answer under a Bodhi tree (pipal tree) in **Bodhgaya**. Enlightened, Gautam Buddha started preaching peace and detachment from desires. The Buddhist festivals are always marked with calm, serenity, and chants. On the Buddha Purnima day, the Buddhists go to the monasteries or **Chaityas** and chant prayers. They offer flowers, candles, and incense sticks, representing the three Buddhist ideals of **Buddha, Dharma, and Sangha.** They also worship stupas, which are said to enshrine a portion of the bone relics of the Buddha.

The concept of image worship was introduced five centuries after the Buddha's death by the Buddhist followers. A Buddhist is also supposed to visit the holy places of **Lumbini, Bodhgaya, Sarnath, Sanchi and Kushinagar**. The Bodhi or peepal tree is also worshipped by decorating it with flower garlands, lighting lamps, and sprinkling milk and scented water on the roots of the tree.

Another important Buddhist celebration is the **Kaza Festival** of Ladakh held in the month of June. Here the Dalai Lama is worshipped as the living incarnation of Lord Buddha. People do a mask dance on this day to frighten away evil spirits.

IMMACULATE OBSERVANCE

(Sabitri)

The new-moon day, the last day of dark fortnight of the month of "Jestha" is called "Sabitri". It happens normally in the beginning of **"June"** every year. Worship, oblation and religious observance are celebrated on this day. Married ladies, celebrate this immaculate observance for the good health, long life and good fortune of their husbands. From the days of yore, the "Vow of Sabitri" is prevalent in Hindu society.

Some of the ladies perform this worship beside a banyan tree. Some perform in their house by bringing a branch of banyan tree. Others worship a pestle—stone (Sila-pua or Sil-batta) as a symbol of "Devi Sabitri". The stone is given water bath by "Panchamrita" which is a mixture of milk, curd, ghee, honey and sugar. Then vermilion, collyrium (Kajal) is applied on it. A sari (woman draping fabric) and some ornaments were put over it. A Brahmin priest is also involved for worshipping Sabitri Devi and doing oblation. Ladies also visit nearest temple to celebrate the occasion, some of them do it at the holy basil plant (Tulsi) of their community and others celebrate it at their home.

In most of the families it is performed at their home. As per the custom, father of the married daughter every year sends fruits, sari, bangles etc through messengers for observance of the 'Sabitri' festival by her daughter. Those who live far away from their native place, the father of the married girl / woman sends money through bank / post office / money order etc.

As per tradition the husband has to make his presence before the wife on this day. The wife invites at least 5 to 7 neighbouring ladies to her house. Photo of famous Deity "Lakshmi-Narayan" couple is kept on a stool. She arranges all the materials such as bangles, bracelets, ornaments, vermillion, collyrium (Kajal), red-dye, new sari and large variety of fruits such as Mango, Jackfruit, Pineapple, Banana, Nuts, Green Gram, Apple, Pear, Grapes, Guava, Orange, Pomegranate, Custard-Apple, Plums, Kiwi, Wood-Apple, Coconut, Cucumber, Cherry, Papaya, Berry, Watermelon, Sugarcane, Dates, Palm Fruit etc for worship. In the beginning, Lord Ganesh, Sun, Bishnu, Shiva, Durga are welcomed to a water-filled pitcher having a coconut upon it and are adored by all. Burning incense, scented sticks, aromatic vapour, resin fumes, lighting ghee lamps, flowers, garlands, propitiatory food and the fruits are offered to the Gods.

At the end of worship, the religious booklet / eulogy, 'Sabitri-Vow' with the episode of the famous immaculate lady Sabitri describing her pledge for the life of husband is read out. All the ladies attending the worship listen to the same. "Sabitri Debi" was powerful, sacred, flawless and character-ful lady. Although she knew the definite death of her husband (Satyavan) in a short period, she willingly married him. She took vow and worshipped "Lakshmi-Narayan" with full devotion for longevity of her husband.

Being aware of Satyavan's certainty of death, she accompanied him to the forest and was observing her vow of worshipping the Gods "Lakshmi Narayan". While Satyaban was cutting woods on a tree, he fell ill; he came down and slept in the laps of Sabitri and died while sleeping. After her husband's death on this new-moon day, the God "Yamraaj" arrived to take Satyavan's soul from Sabitri. She prayed and pleased the God of Death "Yamraaj" and got his boons. By dint of such Sabitri's boons, she achieved miracles such as she could bring back the soul of her dead husband and made him alive. Her issueless father was then blessed by a son; her blind father-in-law got back his eye sight as well as his lost kingdom. Therefore, the main celebrity, "Sabitri Devi" is the icon for all married ladies who remember her vow on this day and celebrate the occasion religiously.

At the end of worship all ladies offer flowers in folded palms (Pushpanjali) to the Gods. After this celebration, the fruits and propitiatory foods (Prasad) are distributed to all ladies. Ladies observing fast for the day take this "Prasad" and go back to their house. Then every husband in the house graces his wife by applying sindoor in simant / maang in following manner.

Sindoor in Simant / Maang: Soon after performing the above Sabitri puja, the wife worships the husband and the husband offers prayers to Gods with folded hands. The wife wears new sari, bangles, ornaments and vermillion which were worshipped in Sabitri Puja. After wearing those, she comes closer to the husband and adores him with her goodwill by genuflecting before him. With heartfelt gratitude he accepts wife's feelings and slowly lifts her up by both hands.

Immediately after standing she brings the small new vermillion box, opens the cover and offers him to grace her by applying vermillion on the parting line of her hair (Simant / Maang). He then takes out the vermillion from the box and smears it on her parting line of fore-head (Simant) by his finger as a mark of chastity. In Hindu belief, the mark of vermillion on fore-head (Simant) is the symbol of chastity for a married lady.

In Hindu families, tradition of observance of "Sabitri Newmoon" is celebrated by couples every year on this day.

DIVINE WEDDING

(Shital Sasthi)

The sixth day of bright fortnight of Jyestha month in 1st week of June is called "Sheetal Shashti" indicating beginning of coolness after scorching heat of the month of May. People eagerly await cool days after facing hot summer days. This is a great festival of Lord Shiva whose marriage ceremony is performed with Goddess Parvati. Since 6th century, this is being celebrated in famous Shiva temples. On the 5th bright day, the marriage is solemnized and on the 6th day, Lord Shiva with wife Parvati returns to his own temple house.

According to the legend, Lord Shiva was to marry his loving lady 'Sati'. But Sati sacrificed her life by self immolation. After knowing death of 'Sati' Lord Shiva became furious and there was no alternative to cool down Him except making him marry to Parvati who was a lover of Lord Shiva. All the Gods had performed this marriage and as a result, Lord Shiva could be cooled down on this day. Two aged Brahmins become father of Shiva and Parvati respectively and 3rd Brahmin acts as Lord Vishnu's representative mediating the marriage. The famous festival of 'Sheetal Shasthi', the divine marriage is conducted with feasts, foods, dowries, lightings, crackers, musical instruments, various dances and grand procession by thousands of mob. The procession travels in the town halting at prominent squares and demonstrating competition of music and dances on the way. Western Odisha enjoys 'Sheetal Shashti' up to the fullest.

As per popular belief, whoever witnesses this divine wedding deserves Lord Shiva's mercy and gets rid of all of his sins.

FESTIVE EARTH

(Raja Festival)

The first day of month "Ashadh" is called "Raja Sankranti". This appears on **Mid-June** every year. The festival of "Raja" is celebrated for 3 consecutive days in a grand manner in coastal districts and middle parts of Odisha. The first day of Raja is called 'Pehli Raja' which appears on last day of month of "Jestha". The 2nd day is 'Raja Sankranti' and the 3rd day is 'Bhumi Dah'.

According to epics, the earth in this period becomes menstruated (Rajavati). It is ready for reproducing crops. "Raja" is a popular festival relating to earth which is compared to a lady. During the three "Raja" days, all sections of people specially the virgin girls celebrate it. In early morning of "Pehli Raja" the girls get up, take bath and assemble at one of their house for undergoing make-up ceremony known as "Sajbaj" (Dressing). The elderly ladies of house assemble there to carry out make-up of the girls. Ornaments, Sandal paste, scented oil, powder, perfume etc are applied on their face and bodies. Combing of hair with different hair styles fitting to each one is done. After make-up, they get well dressed by wearing new saris. The sister-in-laws (Bhabhi) used to take active parts in doing make-up to the family girls.

The girls do not touch the earth by bare feet. They wear new clothes, new shoes and move round in groups to their relatives, neighbours and friends. They are not allowed to undertake any physical work at home. The girls along with small kids in groups are invited by neighbours and relatives to dine in their house. They take delicious food, cakes, curries, juice, syrup, fruits, and sweets etc. For more invitations, the girls are even required in a day to adjust up to 3 houses for 3 times lunch and other 3 houses for 3 times dinner. They enjoy by playing various games like playing-cards, Lido, Chess, Carom and Swinging by cradles along with companions.

Most attractive part of 'Raja' is the 'sporting by swinging' in the hanging cradle. Some people set up hanging cradle at their balcony / veranda, others in their garden by suspending it from the mango tree tying with its branches. In this swing of the garden, most of them sit and swing turn by turn. During swinging, the girls and their companions sing together popular swinging-songs. There are several types of swings and cradles which are utilized according to individual's choice. Young boys with their friends also celebrate the festival by swinging. Some expert swinging players used to swing fast by pose of leaning-up and down and reaching to the ultimate height. Swaying and waving in the swing is a delightful event of the 'Raja' festival.

Prior to "Raja" farmers plough their land and sow the paddy seeds. The main aim of the festival is to allow them leisure from their hard routine work and bring joy and exaltation to their life creating interest and vigour.

Rainy season starts in Odisha from this day (Raja Sankranti). "Raja" festival welcomes the clouds to harmonise with the earth. The seeds under the soil produce seedlings by coming in contact with rain water. 'Raja' initiates the natural sprouting of grains, converting the dry arid lands, paddy fields and pastures into beautiful greeneries.

Boys and elderly men taking leisure from their day to day busy activities, rejoice in games of "Kabaddi", cards, dice etc. They do competition in games among themselves. During the games, drums, trumpets are played by rural artists synchronizing the rhythm with the speed of game. Beating of pair of "Kettle Drum" (Jodi Nagra) is the age old tradition during the game of "Kabaddi". In a competitive game, the winner is given reward by the villagers. The scene and the sound along with the game are very attractive and enjoyable.

It is a grand official holiday in the state. Pleasure visit to the houses of relatives and neighbours is a tradition. Another special attraction of

'Raja' is preparation of beetle-leaf (Paan) in every house and chewing by all. The beetle-leaf is specially prepared with beetle-nuts (supari), spices, lime-paste, catechew-paste (Katha), Clove (Laung), Cardamum (Ilaichi), Coconut power, Fruit preserves, Mint, Mukhwas, Fenel seeds (Saunf), Rose petel preserves (Gulkand) and Candied spices to taste delicious and is offered to the people who visit the house.

Celebration in the form of feast, picnic, parties and get-together takes place among the youths. Generally, non-veg items preferably mutton is prepared in houses during the festival. Due to popular demand of 'Khasi meat' (Castrated Goat) the business of 'Khasi' flourishes. People make queue near the butcher to get their preferred piece of meat. Therefore, price of mutton goes high in these days.

Baked Cake (Pod Pittha): Preparation of delicious "Baked cake" in every house is another speciality of 'Raja'. Powdered raw rice and water in a pot mixed with crushed coconut, molasses and spices are boiled by placing over an oven. Layer of this mixed boiled paste of about 2 inch thick is spread in an earthen circular pot. The surface is then covered by banana leaf over which pieces of burning / smouldering fire are kept to bake the cake. After completion of baking, the cake is removed, cleaned and cut by knife into pieces and served to all family members and the visiting guests. Now days, some people are preparing it by baking inside the pressure cooker.

As per the ritual, the menstruated earth after remaining 3 days untouchable is made to take a sacred bath on 4th day, which is known as "Mother Earth's bathing" (Basumati Snan) or "Mother Laxmi's bathing". Laxmi, the Goddess of fortune is adorned with offering of cakes, fruits and uttering of eulogy. In early morning, the ladies get engaged in preparing for worshipping of the mother earth. The ground in the courtyard is cleaned, mopped and smeared with holy cow-dung water. A wooden low height stool cleaned and washed with water is kept over the smeared ground. Cultivating articles such as plough, yoke, hoe, dagger and crowbar are kept there for worshipping. Grains such as grams, mustard, paddy, cotton and few cooking tools, pestle stone, flowers, sandal paste, vermillion, collyrium, ghee-lamp, incense etc are kept on the stool for adoration. Ladies perform the worship to 'Mother Earth' and offer these with due respect. All family members assemble there, pray and bow down touching their foreheads to the ground seeking blessings from mother earth for good harvest in that year.

'Raja Festival' is celebrated irrespective of caste, creed and age. By the tradition of society, people of each caste from their busy life in the village get these 3 days as holidays in a year. After performing the above worship on 4th day, all the villagers come back again to daily activity and start their farming by using cultivating tools.

CAR FESTIVAL

(Rath Yatra)

In the month of "Ashaadh", on second day of lunar fortnight of **July** Lord Jagannath's Car Festival (Rath Yatra) takes place.

In popular belief, people in Eastern India have great desire to see this auspicious 'Rath Yatra' to get rid of their sins and rebirth. Millions of people travel from distance places and assemble at Puri to have a glimpse of this world famous 'Car Festival'. People of higher status, affluent and rich prefer to purchase ticket of VIP sitting place on the roof of the buildings beside the grand wide road (Bad Dand) of Puri. One can see thousands of people sitting at the roof top of all buildings on either side of the grand road covering a length of 3.5 Kms. All other people, devotees, general public assemble on the grand road (Bad Dand). Huge arrangement by the government is made by deploying thousands of police staff, health workers and volunteers. Devotees of various religious faiths, spirituals organizations, cultural institutions, NGOs, tourists, media persons, ladies, students and children gather in 'Bad Dand'. It is a colourful picturesque scene of kilometres.

Three giant chariots one for 'Lord Jagannath', one for his elder brother 'Balabhadra' and another for his sister 'Subhadra' stand on the grand road in front of the temple. All of them are gorgeously decorated. Jagannath's Car (Chariot) called **"Nandighosh"** of 23 hands height is dressed with yellow cloth having 16 big wheels, 4 white wooden horses one presiding deity accompanied with several Gods at the sides, few more Gods at the entrance and one Charioteer.

Balabhadra's car called **'Taladhwaj'** of 22 hands height is dressed with blue cloth having 14 big wheels, 4 black horses, one presiding deity, several surrounding gods, other gods at the entrance and one Charioteer.

Subhadra's car called **'Darpa Dalan'** of 21 hands height is dressed with red cloth having 12 big wheels, 4 horses, several side goddesses, other goddesses at the entry door and a charioteer. 'Sudarshan', the 4th deity of the main temple (Sri Mandir) has a seat in this chariot near to Subhadra's throne.

At first, god 'Sudarsan', then 'Balabhadra', then 'Subhadra' and lastly 'Jagannath', one after another are carried by the priests from the 'Sri Mandir', in a grand arrival procession known as **'Pahandi'**. Each of them is having big crown made of flowers holding on the head. 'Pahandi' means walking step by step with pace is a customary unique style of lifting and carrying the deity. The arrival procession of Pahandi is very attractive. King of Puri sitting in a palanquin which is carried by men on their shoulders; arrive near the chariots. He gets down having a warm welcome by the Priests who accompany him to Balabhadra's chariot by stepping over the upward approach-ramp. Now the historical famous sweeping ceremony takes place. On the chariot, the King by himself holding the golden broom performs the sweeping and cleaning of the floor of the chariot circling round the deity. Priests following him sprinkle holy rose-scented water on the floor. The King performs scavenging activity in the chariots of Subhadra and then of Jagannath in similar manner.

After this, preparation of pulling activity of the chariot starts by removing the sloped approach-ramp, stretching the pulling ropes and forming a police cordon around the chariot. Anxious devotees struggle and push themselves to come near the chariot and touch the sacred rope for pulling. Ultimately, a large number of police maintain the discipline. Devotees remaining in lines pull the ropes and roll the chariot while singing the traditional pulling-song accompanied with the music of sounding of beating hundreds of gongs, conchs, chorus, loudly pronouncing God's admire, inarticulate ladies' tunes (Hula-Huli) and being excited by high emotions. This is an attractive eye-catching moment involving millions of devotees of different castes, creeds, cults and religions when the chariot journeys towards the 'Gundicha temple'.

Pulling of Subhadra chariot followed by Jagannath chariot is performed in similar way. Colourful promenades accompanying the large chariots and swarms of admiring crowds follow the Grand Road (Bada Dand), overflowing with religious Diaspora. To complete the picture of the carnival; fairs are set up in various corners of the town where the common people gather to celebrate the Car Festival (Rath Yatra). The surrounding is full of colour, vitality, drama and presents a spectacular kaleidoscope.

Thus, on this auspicious occasion, Lord Jagannath accompanied with his siblings armed with Sudarshan leaves the sanctum of the "Sri Mandir" and journeys to the Gundicha Temple sited about 3 kilometres north of the "Sri Mandir". After 8 days stay at Gundicha, the deities return back to the sacrosanct sanctums of the "Sri Mandir" which is known as Return-Car-Festival (**Bahuda Yatra**).

All of these gala arrangements are done to pay a tribute to the Lord and seek his benedictions. The celebrations are a wondrous montage of the bucolic and tribal cultures and interspersed with traces of the classical as well as urban sophistry that holds up the socio-cultural essence of the Indian civilization. Huge 3 chariots pulled by thousands of people, irrespective of religion, caste and creed proclaims their universality and accessibility to humanity at large. Cleaning of chariots by the King with a golden broom indicates that he is the first of Lord's servants and on this particular day he performs the duty of scavenger to demonstrate socialism in action and the dignity of labour.

'Rath Yatra', one of the most significant Odishan festivals, is known by a variety of nomenclature. There are several legends and surmises concerning the supernatural powers of the deities enshrined in the temple. It is said a mere glimpse of the 'Vaman' or the dwarf-form (Lord Jagannath) during the auspicious ceremony frees the devotee from all earthly bonds and helps him attain salvation.

Teej Festival

'Teej' a seasonal festival is celebrated in northern Indian states of Rajasthan, Punjab, Haryana, Delhi, Uttarakhand, Uttar Pradesh and Bihar; heralding the onset of the monsoon season after the season of oppressive heat. It is a festival of womenfolk and is celebrated on 3rd day of the waxing phase of moon (Shukla Paksha) in the month of 'Shravan' **(July-August)**. The festival is named after a small, beautiful, red insect 'Teej' which comes out of the soils during rains.

The girls and women on this day go to the temple after taking bath and offer prayers to Lord Shiva's consort, Goddes Parvati. They also perform 'puja' at home. Commemorating Goddess Parvati's union with Lord Shiva, the festival is celebrated for marital bliss, well being of spouse and children and purification of own body and soul. The festival is a three day long celebration that combines sumptuous feasts as well as rigid fasting.

Female members of family especially daughters are given gifts and dresses. All girls apply **'Mehendi'** or 'Henna' on their hands and wear new bangles, bindies. Married girls go to their mother's house for feast and fun and get gifts from their parents. Swings are hung from trees put up in gardens and grounds. Young girls, women entertain by sitting in the swing, they sway back and forth, sing and dance in the rain with much zest.

Teej gives a chance to women to express their love and devotion for their husband. They observe fast, keep on oil lamp burning all night for the long life of their husbands in earnest devotion, feel closer and more committed to them. Husbands feel more special while watching their wife straining themselves. They reciprocate by being more loving and caring towards their wives. In return, they present beautiful gifts to them as a token of love and become more sensitive towards their doting wives. Mother-in-laws give the newly married daughter-in-law a piece of jewellery on her first Teej after marriage.

Delicious dishes, **'Ghewar'** sweets are prepared during the festival. Eating **'Chat'** from Chaatwallahs is a popular tradition. Many fairs (Melas) are organised with opening of various shops, stalls selling bangles, clothes and eatables.

Rain Swept New Moon

(Chitau Amabasya)

The rainy new moon day of 'Shravan' at the end of **July** is celebrated as 'Chitau Amabasya'. Trinity of Lord Jagannath at Puri are decorated by colours marked on their foreheads wearing precious ornaments as diamond, gold, neelam, ruby etc called as **'Chita'** (Variegation). Therefore, the festival all over the state is known as 'Chitalagi' or 'Chitau Amabasya'. Most of the people of village being cultivators they do transplantation of paddy by planting seedlings in their fields during this rainy season. This is an agricultural festival where farmers worship the paddy fields. On this occasion, a special rice-cake called **'Chitau Pitha'** (Variegated Cake) is prepared and offered to the deity, to the corn field and aquatic animals.

All ladies in villages prepare this cake by special technique. A paste is prepared by grinding raw rice and tender coconut. Cheese, molasses and salt are added to the paste. A flat pan (Tawa) is kept over an oven and thin layer of cooking oil is applied on the surface of the pan. Then it is heated and a bowl of the paste is poured and spread over the heated surface of the pan making it circular shape. It is then covered by another plate and is left to be baked. After sometime, the plate is removed and the variegated baked cake is ready to be served. The cake is never turned back to bake its other side. The cake is taken by farmers to the paddy field with other holy materials. The paddy field considered as Goddess 'Mahalaxmi' is worshipped with these offerings.

It is popularly believed that devotional offering of 'Chitau Pitha' to the field will have good harvest of crops. Many also believe that taking 'Chitau Pitha' on this day keeps one hale and hearty throughout the year. Another significant event is worshipping the snails in the water and praying them to avoid their wrath. Snails breed enormously in the paddy fields and ponds during the rainy season. Farmers while working barefooted in the fields often get their feet cut by the sharp edge of their shells. 'Chitau Pitha' is broken to small pieces and is thrown into the water of corn fields, ponds, canals and river for feeding the snails. People believe that the snails will not bite their legs while the farmers working in bare foot in the watery field.

Children accompanying their friends in villages carry the cake and sit besides water of the small irrigating canals. They throw pieces of cake to the water to feed the aquatic animals, those swim towards the bank to take the food. The pleasant experience of getting drenched with friends remaining outside from the house in rainy days; observing the slow movement of the snails and carefully catching them; playing with them thinking that they will not cut their skin; the scene of fast moving group of fishes approaching the shore for eating the cake and then quickly going away are unforgettable memories. The neighbouring ladies distribute these cakes with other holy offerings among each other. Some people believe that the offering of 'Chitau Pitha' to water is to please 'Water-God' who will be happy to protect us from flood.

Another belief is the evil spirit appearing in darkness of the rainy new moon night visits houses to suck blood from our kids. Therefore, the mother makes a mark around the navel of the child by drawing peculiar designs or cauterizes it. The cake is first offered to the evil spirit to be appeased and thereafter it is served in the family.

People think by praying and worshipping animals, birds, trees and reptiles, they can get rid of all dangers. Snails-worshipping is the indication of such trust. Preparation of 'Chitau Pitha' (Chitau Cake) is delicious and healthy. Taking cakes are more beneficial in comparison to taking rice. Therefore, in most of the festivals, cakes are prepared and offered to Gods and then are served as proprietary food to everyone.

Sacred Thread Of Love

(Raksha Bandhan)

The full moon of 'Shravan' month, around middle of **August** is called 'Rakshi Purnima' or 'Raksha Bandhan or 'Gamha Purnima'.

Raksha Bandhan is a festival about affection, fraternity and sublime sentiments in India. This is a 'bond of protection' by the brother to his sister who ties, the sacred thread of love, **'Rakshi'** on his wrist. This is an occasion to flourish love, care, affection and sacred feeling of brotherhood. It symbolizes the sister's love and prayers for her brother's well being and the brother's life long vow to protect her.

Sisters tie Rakshi on the wrist of their brothers amid chanting of mantras, put roli and rice on his forehead and pray for his well-being. She bestows him with gifts and blessings. In turn, brothers also wish her a good life and pledges to take care of her. He gives her a return gift. The gift symbolizes the physical acceptance of her love, reminder of their togetherness and his pledge.

It is an opportunity to reunion and celebrates. People also share tasty dishes, wonderful sweets and exchange gifts. It is a time to share their past experiences also. For those who are not able to meet each other, Rakshi cards e-Rakshis and colourful rakshis made of thread are sent through mails / posts with loving Rakshi massages. Handmade Rakshi and self-made Rakshi cards are representation of the personal feelings of the siblings.

Other than natural relations, girls and ladies also establish brotherly relation with any close person of their choice by tying Rakshi on this day. The adopted brother rewards the newly made sister and promises to protect her in difficulties.

On this day, as per epics, Goddess Laxmi has tied Rakshi to the eminent, generous king Bali. Pandava's mother Kunti had tied Rakshi to the hands of Lord Krishna to protect her sons from the oppression of Kauravas. The ladies of 'Gop Puri' had tied Rakshi to Lord Krishna with loving wishes. As per history, Rajput ladies in order to save their chastity, used to tie Rakshi in the hands of Muslim kings ruling them. The emperor Akbar used to support & celebrate by giving priority to the festival of Rakshi.

Gahma-Purnima: Rakshi Purnima is also known as Gahma Purnima in rural places of eastern India. Villagers celebrate it by worshipping their cattles which is their main support in cultivation. The walls and floors of cattle house (cowshed) are cleaned by water. Ladies decorate the walls of cowshed drawing artistic figures by using the liquefied rice-paste. The mud walls of houses in villages are painted by such rice-water. Cows, oxen, calves are washed, cleaned by bathing them with soap-water. Sandal paste, vermilion is applied on the forehead of every cattle. Each cattle's neck is decorated with flower garland. The oxen are covered by new cloths. All give caress to each one of the cattle and food is served to them. After this, they are worshipped religiously. It is believed that all the Gods reside in the body of a cow; hence they are treated with high esteem.

In good old days 'Gahma Jumping' (Cow jumping) was observed in the society. People used to make a small statue of an ox out of clay and a male calf was made to jump or cross over the same which is called as 'Gahma jumping' (Cow-jumping) which is almost forgotten and lost in the society. To commemorate this old tradition, 'Gahma Jumping' is observed at some villages. A gate-way portal with two supporting pillars on the ground is made on upland. A packet having coconut, cloth, cash etc is made to hang from the portal. One has to run from a distance and jump at the portal to touch the packet.

Brahmins, priests visit houses to make the family members wear a long white sacred thread from neck to the waist and chant hymns reciting names of seven long lived famous celebrities of Indian epics. They tie wrists of the family members with red coloured holy threads as God's protection and bless to live long.

'Balram' the elder brother of Lord Jagannath was born on this day. Some people celebrate his birth day by making a sleeping statue of Balram out of clay holding a plough and a mace and worshipping him with fire oblation. In all temples of Lord Jagannath and Lord Bishnu, the statue of Radha Krishna is kept in cradle and made to swing in a swinging ceremony of enjoying rainy seasons. The impressive swinging ceremony at Jagannath Puri is performed with pomp and luxuries. Artistic decoration by skilled artists, their high standard paintings, drawings and sculptures are visible in this.

EID-UL-FITR

Eid-Ul-Fitr popularly known as Eid is the most auspicious festival observed by the muslim community to celebrate the conclusion of the month of fasting, Ramzan (Ramadan).

Ramzan symbolizes a lots of practices and beliefs of the community. It is for restraining oneself from having food and to abstain from all kinds of evil and unlawful practices in Islam. The practice of fasting also known as **Roza** that starts from the break of dawn till dusk and during this whole day, an individual has to refrain himself from drinking, eating and maintaining celibacy. The month long fasting ends with the festival of **Eid-ul-Fitr** that symbolizes a reward for their fasting.

The festival of **Eid** is celebrated on the first day of the next month namely **Shawwal**, the tenth month of the Hijra calendar which starts when three people sight the new moon. It is believed that Prophet Mohammad offered prayer to Allah or God, observed fast for whole month of Ramzan as a penance seeking forgiveness for the sins of mankind and went on praying and meditating. The Holy Quran, the Islamic religious book, was revealed to him by Allah during this period and Prophet was asked to spread his message amongst people.

During the Eid festival, Muslims exchange gifts, greeting their neighbours as a mark of solidarity and brotherhood. Devotees wear new clothes and go to the mosque for prayers. Everybody lines up in the open courtyard to offer **namaz**. People also give alms or **zakaat** to the poor.

After the rituals, the feasts and fairs start, Fairs are organised everywhere and large feasts are also organised. People decorate their houses and prepare luscious traditional sweets and cuisines to celebrate the festival. The most common recipe in this festival is the delicious **Meethi Seviyan / Sewain**(Sweet Vermicelli) prepared from various healthy and mouth-watering ingredients. Gifts are also exchanged and elders give money, called **idi**, to children. It is a festival that brings gifts, feasts, and joy. Greeting cards are sent featuring the words **"Eid Mubbarak"** (Blessed Eid). It combines the rituals and traditions of the religion with the fun and frolic of everyday life.

The significance of this festival is interpreted as a good time to bring people together in harmony and gratitude.

Virgin's Solemnity

(Khuda Rukuni)

The festival known as 'Khudarukuni' (Khuda-loving) is celebrated by the virgins in the villages of coastal districts of eastern India in the moth of Bhadrab on all 5 Sundays. The month of Bhadrab covers some part of **August** as well as **September**. Goddess 'Durga' is the presiding deity in this celebration. She likes the **baked-broken-rice** called **'Khuda'**, therefore the name is Kuda-loving-festival. In early morning village girls collect flowers and go to take bath in village pond. After having bath, they build small temples by sand and clay beside the pond and decorate those by flowers. They pay their first respect to the goddess as if living in these hand made temples by them. They return home and keep on fasting through out the day.

A covered space is chosen for worship. The out-house of pedal block (Dhinki) for husking paddy is preferred. Neighbouring families assemble here for community worshipping of 'Khudarukuni'. All of them with their virgin girls arrive at evening and celebrate the occasion. This house is cleaned and washed. The floor is mopped by holy cow dung water and is decorated by carving and drawing different designs using liquefied rice paste.

A large quantity of flowers is collected from the village. Various flowers like rose, china-rose, water lily, champak, oleander, flower of thorn apple etc are used in the worship. Garlands are prepared by the girls and the place is beautifully decorated by flowers. The statue of the Goddess or the image of Goddess made of flowers and leaves is established at that place and is worshipped by the girls using ghee-lamps, incense, flowers, vermillion etc. Baked-broken-rice (Khuda), cucumber, parched paddy and sweet-parched-paddy, coconut etc are offered as "Prasad".

First part of the ceremony described in the book is the appearance of the Goddess Durga and the episode of her manifestation in killing the wicked demon 'Mahisasur'. People believe that the girls will derive powers from the Goddess and shall be able to eradicate miseries and troubles of mankind like the Goddess Durga.

In the second part of ceremony at the end of worship, the story of a virgin named 'Taapoi', with the eulogy is read out by the group. Ladies, girls and children attending the festival become devotionally attached and listen to it carefully.

'Taapoi' was the daughter of a merchant having 7 brothers and 7 daughter-in-laws. As she was a fond child of the family, her father was fulfilling all her desires. She wanted to build a big moon made of gold which her father started making, but before completion of the same, both the parents died. In course of time, the family became poor and all 7 brothers left by boat through the ocean to foreign countries for trading. While going they handed over their loving sister 'Taapoi' to their wives and advised them to take care of her. After they had left, one wicked widow lady often visiting their house influenced these ladies against 'Taapoi', blaming her as the root cause of misfortunes. They treated her inhumanly, gave lot of troubles and tortured. She was ill-faid and sent to the forest for grazing their goats. Only the youngest daughter-in-law was liking her but could not much help in fear of others.

'Taapoi', in the midst of miseries was worshipping the Goddess 'Durga' and was praying for quick return of her brothers. She joined group of girls and worshipped the Goddess offering the baked-broken-rice (Khuda) as a result of which her brothers returned safely and landed at the sea shore at midnight incidentally nearer to her. The brothers could listen her weeping from a distance, reached there and discovered her. After gathering the facts from Taapoi; the brothers became angry and punished 6 wives by cutting their noses leaving only the good youngest one. Later on, by the noble worship of Tapoi, the goddess Durga cured their noses.

The celebration comes to an end and the food-offering are taken by all. After worshipping on 5 Sundays, the statue of goddess is then taken by the group to the pond / river for immersion. Aim of the festival is to make the virgins powerful like Durga and develop tolerance to face troubles with patience like that of 'Taapoi'. The brave, undaunted, enduring character provides happiness in life

BIRTH OF DIVINITY

(Janmashtami)

The 8th day of dark fortnight in the month of 'Bhadrab' is called as 'Janmashtmi' which is significant as birth day of Lord Krishna. This happens normally in the month of **August** every year. In Mathura, Brindaban, famous Krishna temples, in all Jagannath temples; this festival is celebrated with great pomp. This is very auspicious festival in all families in India. God manifests Himself in different incarnations to kill the wicked and establishes the virtue. Out of 10 incarnations, Lord Krishna is taken as one incarnation.

On this day Krishna was born in a prison at Mathura from His mother 'Devki'. His father 'Vasudev' and mother 'Devki' were imprisoned by his wicked uncle King 'Kansa' (Devki's brother) who was killing all the new born babies of Devki because of a forecast to him that the 8th son of Devki will kill him. At night, when the 8th child, Lord Krishna was born, the dark prison got lighted by divine light. The prison doors opened themselves and the guards fell in deep sleep and could not notice the advent of new born. Vasudev's chains and handcuffs got freed and he was released by divine power. Vasudev out of fear of killing by 'Kansa' kept the new born Krishna in a basket and carried it on his head and walked to 'Gopa Pur' (Gokul). This was a dark, rainy day when river Yamuna was in flood. Protected by the hood of the great serpent 'Ananta' of Lord Vishnu, he crossed the flooded river carrying Krishna on his head. On the way, due to God's blessing the flooded deep water gave way to him and he reached Gokul safely.

After arriving at Gokul, he handed over Krishna to the King 'Nanda' and his wife Yashoda and instead, carried back Yashoda's new born daughter to Mathura. Kansa after knowing the birth of 8th child of Devki as daughter, he lifted the girl and smashed on a stone to kill her. But she being a divine soul, vanished away by cautioning Kansa that his killer is being brought up in Gokul. Later on, Kansa has tried to kill 'Krishna'. Even after several attempts; he could not kill Lord Krishna for His infinite divine power. Ultimately, Kansa was killed by Lord Krishna.

Therefore, birth of Lord Krishna is an auspicious occasion and is celebrated throughout the country as 'Janmashtami'. People keep fasting until Krishna's birth at midnight and up to finishing of His worship by the Priest. All devotees arrive in the nearby Krishna temple carrying fruits and sweets for offering of "Prasad". The Priest eulogize the birth episode of Lord Krishna from the epics. Assembled persons listen to the poetic descriptions attentively with devotional satisfaction awaiting Krishna's auspicious birth at midnight.

On Janmashtmi day, all devotees arrive at night at their local 'Krishna Temple' / 'Bhagbat Ghar'/ 'Jaggannath temples' to celebrate birthday of Lord Krishna. They observe the day without taking any food (fasting). The priest arrives at evening for performing religious activities. Each family brings fruits, sweets, flowers, incense etc in a wicker-basket for worshipping Krishna. The epic 'Bhagbat' or the 'Haribansh' is read out depicting birth events of Lord Krishna and his activities at Gokul.

Everywhere during Puja ceremony, the chapter narrating the birth event is read loudly by the priest with attractive rhythm and devotees listen carefully. Episode of Krishna's birth event is read out matching the time just at midnight, as Lord Krishna was born at that time. When the birth event of Krishna is narrated, out of happiness, all raise their voice at a time welcoming the Lord's arrival. They praise the Lord sounding His holy names with emotion. Conches, gongs, bells etc are sounded simultaneously with their praising chorus. The priest performs the religious activities and offers food to the God. An idol of Krishna in his baby form is kept in a cradle and the devotees take turns pulling its string to rock the baby Krishna. Those devotees undergoing fasting throughout the day as a religious observance (Vow), they now break their fast and take food after Krishna's birth occurrence and worship at midnight. Each devotee collects his / her basket of "Prasad" (Propitiatory food) and returns home. King 'Nanda' had celebrated Krishna's birthday on the next day. Therefore, the race of milkmen in India celebrates **'Nand Uschhav'** on that day.

Cultural events like 'Krishna Leela' and **'Ras Leela'** are organized at some places. In the state of Maharashtra, **'Dahi Handi'** (Curd Vessel) event is organized. Young men and boys form a human pyramid and try to break earthen pots full of curd or butter suspended high in the sky between houses. The troup gets ample rewards from organizers for performing this.

ONAM

On 12th day of waning phase of moon (Krishna Paksha) in the month of Bhadrab (Bhadrab Krishna Dwadashi), Onam is celebrated in the state of Kerala. It normally falls in early **September** every year. This is the period when the southwest monsoon ends, and the spring and harvest seasons begin in the state.

As per legend, this festival is celebrated to rejoice the homecoming of the King Mahabli to his own state. It is said that King Bali ruled in the state of Kerala. He was a just and benevolent ruler and above all, loved his people. When King Mahabali gained more popularity and wanted to expand the empire further, Lord Vishnu took his incarnation of 'Vamana' form and tried to limit his popularity for being the ultimate in charity. As a dwarf Brahmin (Vamana), Lord Vishnu arrived in the court of King Bali and asked for just three paces of land equivalent to 3 foot-steps. King Bali laughed and immediately granted him the seemingly small wish. The Vamana then assumed his enormous form and in his one step covered the skies, in the second step he took over the whole earth.

When he was waiting to take the third step, the large-hearted Bali put forth his own head to get salvation. Lord Vishnu was pleased and granted Mahabli one last wish. The benevolent king said that he wanted to come back to his land Kerala and visit his people once a year. The Lord granted his wish and placed his third step over Bali's head and took his life. Onam is the day when King Bali comes to visit his people. Inhabitants of Kerala always try to come back to their home place in Kerala from distant lands of their livelihood / employment to meet their own people on this occasion.

On Onam, people decorate their houses and city with flowers and rangoli (coloured paints). They wear new clothes and in a festive mood, perform dances and dramas. For the family feast, special dishes are prepared.

Kerala appears in its grandiose best on this day. Cultural extravaganza, music and feasts add colors of merriment and joy to the 'God's Own Country'. There are celebrations all around the state and everybody takes active participation in them; Onam has assumed a secular character and is celebrated by people of all religions and communities.

Morning Rituals: People wake up as early as 4 am on the day of Onam. Day begins with cleaning of the house. Front courtyards are smeared with cow dung, where the houses are not cemented. On the day of Thiruvonam conical figures in various forms are prepared from sticky clay and are painted red. These are decorated with a paste made of rice-flour and water and are placed in the front court yard and other important places in the house. Some of these clay figures are in the shape of cone and others represent figures of Gods. The tradition of making clay cones (Trikkara Appan) has its roots in mythology, which says that festival originated at Trikkakara, a place 10 km from Cochinand, was the capital in the reign of legendary King Mahabali.

Elaborate prayers ceremonies and pujas are also performed on this day. A senior member of the house plays the role of the priest and conducts the rituals. He wakes up early and prepares rice-flour and molasses for 'Nivedyam' (offerings to God). Lamps are lit up in front of the idols and all members of the house join in for the ceremonies. Priest offers rice-flour, flowers and water in the names of the God. As Onam is also a harvest festival, people thank God for the bountiful harvest and pray for the blessings in the coming year. A peculiar custom is followed after this, wherein male members make loud and rhythmic shouts of joys. The tradition is called, 'Aarppu Vilikkukal'. This represents the beginning of Onam.

It is now the time for members of the house to dress up in their best attire and offer prayers in the local temple. Most people wear new clothes on the day. There is also a tradition of distributing new clothes on Onam. In Tharawads (traditional large family consisting of more than hundred people), Karanavar, the eldest member of the family, gives new clothes as gifts, called 'Onapudava', to all family members and servants. Other members of the family exchange gifts amongst each other.

The Big Feast-Onasadya: After completing the morning rituals, it is time for the family to get ready for the grand meal called Onasadya. The biggest and most prominent place in the house is selected to lay the meal which is traditionally served in a row on a mat laid on the floor. The central place in the row is occupied by the eldest member of the family. In front of him is placed a lighted brass lamp at a distance. Towards the west of the lamp is placed a small plantain leaf on which the food is served. This is an offering made in the name of Lord Ganapathy.

Thereafter, the meal is served to all present. The elaborate meal consists of 11 to 13 strictly vegetarian dishes and is served on banana leaves. There is a fixed order of serving the meal and a set place to serve the various dishes on the leaf. A lot of preparation and hard work goes in making of the scrumptious Onasadya.

Fun-Dances and Games: After the grand meal, it's time for people to indulge in recreational activities and enjoy the festival. Men of strength and vigour go in for rigorous sports while senior members pass time by playing indoor games like chess and cards. There is a set of traditional games to be played on Onam which are collectively called, 'Onakalikal'. It includes ball games, combats, archery and Kutukutu (Kerala version of Kabaddi).

Women go in for dancing activities as there are specific dances like Kaikottikali and Thumbi Thullal for the festival of Onam. Women performing the graceful clap dance called 'Kaikotti Kali' in their traditional gold bordered 'mundu and neriyathu' presents a splendid sight. Besides, there is also a tradition of playing on a decorated swing hung from a high branch. Onappaattu—Onam Songs are also sung on the occasion. Celebrations and cultural programmes are held all across the state to mark the festival of Onam in which a large number of people participate. Prominent amongst them are Vallamkali—the Snake Boat Race and entertaining events like Kummatti kali and Pulikali. The other highpoint of Onam is the dazzling display of fire works. The state of Kerala can be seen engulfed in light and spirit of merriment when people burst patassu or fire crackers.

Boat Race: A unique feature of Onam is the boat race. On this day a race takes place in the backwater lagoons of Kerala. The amazing race attracts tourists from all over the world and brings the festival to a spectacular end.

GOD OF THE MASSES

(Shri Ganesh)

Festival of Ganesh Chaturthi is celebrated on 4th day of waxing phase of moon (Shukla Paksha) in the month of 'Bhadrab' **(Aug-Sept)**. It is also called as 'Binayak Chaturthi' and is celebrated with great fervour in the state of Maharashtra, Gujarat, Andhra Pradesh, Odisha and in some part of other states also. Apart from India, worshipping of Ganesh also takes place in China, Japan, Tibet, Myanmar, Indonesia, Bali, Mexico and America.

As per epics, Lord Shiva who had chopped of Ganesha's head in a fighting without knowing him as his son, had repented and placed the elephant's head on Ganesha's body and infused life in it. Lord Shiva had blessed his son by declaring that he would be Ganapati (Leader of masses), Vighneshwara (queller of all obstacles) and the first to be worshipped amongst the Gods. "Shri Ganesh" is also the phrase used to denote an auspicious beginning of a new project or venture.

In educational institutions the worshipping of Shri Ganesh is done in great grandeur. Students, teachers and guardians together take part in this. It is celebrated in market places, towns, cultural organizations and public places. Intricately designed clay idols of Lord Ganesh are installed in a big stage and are worshipped. The stage and the idol's platform are decorated with coloured papers, flowers and lightings. Writers and businessmen perform the worship with lot of dedication. The devotees observe fasting and wear new clothes. Parents observe this day as commencement of learning of their small children. The child is made to hold a new piece of writing stick (chalk) and learns writing first alphabets. The deity is worshipped with flowers, leaves, doob-grass, fruits, sweets, ladoo and coconut. Breaking of coconut by devotees before Lord Ganesh is a great event. After a week or ten day period of worship and festival the idols of Lord Ganesh is taken in a grand procession by the devotees and immersed in the water of the nearest river or sea.

On this auspicious day, all the schools are declared for study holiday but open for the celebration. Each student contributes cash and is collected by the class monitors. According to the financial condition of the student's family the amount of contribution is decided by the monitor and declares in the class. Within few days the total amount is collected and is deposited to a Puja Committee where representatives of the students and teachers are the members. The committee decides the different aspects, such as decoration, ordering statue, worshipping activities, devotional music, community-feast and immersion ceremony. These are elaborately planned with distribution of responsibility to different committees. Few days before Ganesh Chaturthi become preparation days for various committees. The previous night is spent with long extended duration by committee members for decoration of the school, the stage and the sitting platform of the idol.

On this day, all attend the Puja wearing new dresses and worship Lord Ganesh. The priest arrives at scheduled time. One person is nominated for performing the rituals of worship, remains closely associated with the priest. Supported by other team members he arranges the articles for Puja and sits before Lord Ganesh along with the Priest for sacred offering and oblation. Study materials such as pen, pencil, book, notebook etc are kept beside the Idol for worshipping. The Priest chants loudly the hymns and performs the Puja for several hours. All sit in front of the idol; participate in the puja and oblation praying the God with devotion.

At the end, the priest asks the devotees to stand up and offer prayer to the Lord by holding handful of flower in both hands. He chants the sacred words / hymns loudly and all do repeat those words. This process is repeated three times. After this, everyone bows down and crouches before the Lord. Food-offering (Prasad) is then distributed to all. The group in charge of preparation of meal make sitting arrangements for taking the grand cooked lunch. It is a pleasant event of groups sitting together and taking the food on banana leaf. Till the day of immersion, the deity is worshipped in the pulpit. Soon after finding a suitable time, the immersion procession is arranged. Devotees carry the idol in an open carrier / vehicle to the nearest river with music and amusements. The idol is then lifted and carried into the water and is submerged in to the river.

There is a tradition in India that the statue of Lord Ganesh must be installed besides the main presiding Deity of a temple. Before start of worshipping of any God, the Priest first does invocation to Lord Ganesh and adores Him. The tradition of this worship is very ancient and was started from 5th century. Not only in the Hindu religion but also in Jainism and Budhism Lord Ganesh is worshipped. In Brazil of South America, an ancient statue of Shri Ganesh was found which is of 5000 yrs old.

In the famous temple 'Sri Mandir' at Puri; Lord Jagannath is decorated in the form of an elephant resembling Lord Ganesh on His bathing-full-moon festival (Devasnan Poornima) day which is the day of His investiture.

DIVINE CRAFTSMAN

(Vishwakarma)

The Hindus believe that 'Lord Viswakarma' is the presiding deity of industries, crafts, architecture and engineering. On the 5th day of waning phase of moon in the month of Ashwin **(September)**. He is worshipped by the engineering community, industrial houses, technocrats, artists, workers and craftsmen as a mark of reverence. He provides courage and inspiration to all workers, engineers, manufacturers and designers. Throughout the country, all industries, factories, workshops, manufacturing plants, mills and production units celebrate worshipping of Lord Viswakarma in festive moods.

The Lord sits on the back of his appurtenance (carrier), the elephant and holds in his four hands, a water-pot, the Vedas, a noose and craftsman's tools. Rituals are followed by the distribution of "Prasad". The yearly feast is cooked, where the workmen and the owners take lunch together. Throughout the day colourful kites are flown. The sky fills up with all shades and colours. Workers at many places make resolutions to perform better from this auspicious day. One of the important festivals of India, Vishwakarma Puja is marked with usual gaiety. All the industrial places, shops that engage small or heavy machineries and owners of vehicles aptly summon Lord Vishwakarma, thanking Him for His grace and seeking His blessing in smooth running of their machineries. Pandals come up in busy streets and "Prasad" is distributed to the devotees.

In large industries, Viswakarma is worshipped in each department. Although this is not a declared holiday, practically no work is performed by workers in the factory except emergency works. On this day family members, ladies, relatives and friends are allowed to visit the plant right up to the worshipping place. Now a day, on account of safety and security, most of the industries in India perform the ceremony outside the plant gate or inside the township by constituting joint puja-committee consisting of management and workers. In this, the management of the industry also provides funds and shares the expenditure. At the evening, light decoration, music parties, opera play, concerts, cultural events and dinner parties are performed by the members. Next day, the statue of Lord Vishwakarma is taken for emersion in the nearest river with grand procession and the celebration ends.

PARTAKING NEW GRAIN

(Nabanna)

This festival is celebrated in West-Odisha and East-Chattisgarh on 5th day of bright fortnight of month Bhadrab (**September**). It is believed that on this day by offering the first harvest of the year to the God brings happiness in life, crops grow abundantly and the house gets enriched with wealth.

The harvest festival of **Nabanna** (Nua Khai) which means 'Partaking the new grain' is a very popular ceremony among rice growers of India. In the famous "Samlei" temple at Sambalpur, the Goddess "Samlei" is the presiding diety. She is worshipped with the food-offering of new grain. It typically honours the goddess Lakshmi who symbolises wealth and fertility. In every house the Goddess Lakshmi is worshipped with cleanliness and sanctity. Farmers cut and husk a special variety of rice and typically offer it prepared as rice porridge. Preparation of cakes, feasts, divine worship and family get together is the main activity of 'Nabanna'. According to custom, community cannot enjoy the new rice crop until goddess Lakshmi is first offered Nabanna (New food or new rice)

Mutual respect is observed among different level of family members, relatives and friends. They embrace each other with goodwill and co-operation. Youngsters offer respect and obeisance to the elders and the elders bless the youngsters in return. All members of family wear new clothes and visit their cultivating field carrying articles of worships. They pour milk in their field and worship Goddess Lakshmi for good harvest. In the evening; dance, music and cultural activities take place.

In some parts of the country the partaking (eating) of new grain is celebrated also on Dusshera day and some other parts it is celebrated on Pongal day (Makar Sankranti).

MAHALAYA OBSEQUES

(Shraddh)

The New moon day of month of Ashwin **(September)** is called "Mahalaya". On this day, Hindus offer obsequies (Shraddh) in honour of their ancestors who have already expired. By obsequious rites, people memorise their ancestors and express their obligations to them. In earlier days people used to offer Shraddh upto 14 generations, then it was followed upto 7 generations and now a days it is generally done upto 3 generations. Other than the rite of Shraddh performed on specific death day, this day is granted to observe for all the ancestors. Therefore, this is taken as a popular festival.

The dark fortnight of month of Ashwin upto the Mahalaya new moon day is meant for such offerings. Every day in this period is suitable for oblation to the manes. Apart from own house, the offerings are done in sacred places such as temples and beside river banks. The performer or the contributor (the heir) keeps fasting until performance of 'Shraddh' and takes vegetarian food after wards in his own house or in the temple. Brahmin Priests during these days are abundantly available at such sacred places. One has to take hold of one such priest to perform Shraddh. The priest arranges all materials required for Shraddh. Near-by shops are available selling the ceremonial articles of funeral offering. Banana-leaf, flower, flour, rice, til (Sesamum), vermilion, incense sticks, butter lamps, sacred grasses etc. are all available there.

Shraddh Ritual: The Priest guides the performer (the heir) to prepare moist flour by hand and to keep those on a banana leaf forming several tiny altars named after each ancestor. The Heir is instructed by the Priest how to establish each altar by carrying a portion of moist-flour and pouring on the banana leaf in a specific pose of palm while he (the Priest) simultaneously utters the hymns. One has to remember names of as many generations viz, father, grandfather, great-grand-father, mother, grandmother and great-grand-mother etc of both paternal and maternal generations. Each tiny altar is offered with flower, incense, vermilion, sandal paste, water, waving of burning lamp etc by the performer (the heir) sitting on the specific pose of touching his left knee on the ground. At the end; the proprietary foods of Shraddh is collected by the performer (the heir) and he offers those to available nearby animals like cow, buffalo, dog etc. The Priest is also offered food / meal to take there. He is offered with gifts of some fruits, vegetables, rice etc to carry to his home. Ultimately the Priest is given his dues (Dakshina) by cash and he blesses the performer (the heir) and his family by uttering hymns and pouring rice and flower on the head of each member as they sit in front of him paying their regards.

These obsequies (Shraddh) are known as sacrificial duty towards our ancestors. Normally, people offer this on the death anniversary of their parents. This sacrificial action carries goodness, beneficial to mankind and culminates prosperity.

People perform Mahalaya Shraddh at sacred places such as Gaya of Bihar, Varanasi on bank of river Ganges, Haridwar at Ganges, bank of sacred rivers of India and in the famous Jagannath temple and Shiva temples in India. Lord Jagannath offers 'Shraddh' for his ancestors. It is believed that performing 'Shraddh' by sitting on the 10th, 11th and 12th steps of 'Shri Mandir' (Jagannath temple) is sacred.

DUSSEHRA

(Vijay Dashmi)

I n 2nd and 3rd century Durga Puja had started in Eastern India. Worship of statue made of clay had started since 16th and 17th century. The statue of Durga is made in the pose of her killing the wicked demon king 'Mahishasur' riding over her carrier the lion. Statue of Goddess Lakshmi with her carrier owl, Saraswati with her swan, Ganesh with his mouse, Karthikeya with his peacock and Mahadev with his bull are also made out of clay and placed beside the main statue of goddess Durga. As per epics, getting frightened by the demon Mahishasur all the Gods prayed the Lord-God. Taking the united power and weapons of all the Gods, Goddess Durga was born. Crowned with extraordinary power she could kill 'Mahishasur' and established peace in world.

'Durga' is the goddess to wipe out "Durgati" i.e. troubles. In Eastern part of India, she is worshipped with great grandeur during "Dushera" in the month of **October**. People offer 'Puspanjali" (handful of flower) on all three days of Astami, Navami & Dashami at the nearest community's Durga Puja stage in morning and evening. Ladies offer "Prasad". Our family without fail celebrates this with full austerity. Community children, ladies and gents perform some cultural and devotional song before the goddess every evening.

Invocation by Aarti (Waving of Lamp): Everyday's Puja and 'Aarti' are very much attractive and enjoyable. The rhythm of beating drum known as 'Dhakia' and the Aarti which is performed by waving of lighted earthen lamps, firing resin and burning incense before Goddess-Durga in different dancing poses are unforgettable moments. Turn by turn the devotees perform this Aarti in groups with background sound of Dhakia.

Community Feast (Khechdi Prasad): The Dashmi day is the day for community feast. "Khechdi "Prasad" is served to all who gather there. All sit down on the floor without feeling of cast, creed, designation and level and take food on leaf. Ultimately, on Dashmi day, the statue of goddess is taken for immersion and is submerged in nearby river with grand procession and music.

On this day people worship Durga for acquiring power, knowledge and wealth. In every house people of all caste according to their profession in society worship their professional tools, instruments, weapons, vehicles, books etc. They wear new clothes, cook and dine delicious food, cakes and sweets, invite their relatives. The unique famous cake prepared on this day is called "Manda Cake". People initiate new activities; inaugurate works on this day as it is taken as an auspicious day. Now-a-days every town, city has "Durga Puja" / "Dussehra" committee and permanent stage.

Durga is the goddess which was worshipped by Lord 'Shri Ram' before going to fight with demon-king 'Ravana' & got the blessings to kill him. He got the victory by worshipping 'Durga'. She is the embodiment of destroyers of evils. Therefore, we worship goddess 'Durga' on these days to get blessing from her who will save us from troubles and disasters. During Mahabharat war Lord Krishna had advised Arjun to worship mother Durga for winning the battle.

In the famous Jagannath temple, the goddess 'Bimla' is worshipped in 11 different outfits / dresses during 16 days grand worship up to 'Mahaashtami' and then worship of 'Dussehra' from 'Mahashtami' to 'Dashami'.

Ramleela: During the festival, 'Ramleela' is performed by local artists for about 7 days at night. The episode of 'Shri Ram' in exile, Stealing of Devi 'Sita' by Ravan, conquering Lanka by Shri Ram and killing Ravan in the war are displayed with sound and music. This is very popular, attractive and loved by common people everywhere. On the last Dushmi day the scene of battle of Ram and Ravana with killing of Ravan is performed as the concluding episode of 'Ramleela'.

Burning of Effigy: In the open ground, the statue of 'Ravan', 'Kumbhakaran' and 'Meghnaad' are made out of clothes, bamboo and paper. These are then made to stand erected on the ground. Fire crackers are fitted inside the statues. After the stage-show of killing of Ravan in Ramleela, these statues are finally ignited by the hands of important person of locality. The statues then burn with large fire, huge sound of burning crackers finally get into ashes. By this, people believe that all the troubles and wicked powers are killed, all evils are wiped out thus; virtue is established and will continue to prevail.

YOUTHFUL MOON

(Kumar Purnima)

The full moon night of month of Ashwin **(October)**is called 'Kumar Purnima' which is the tradition of worship by young boys and girls (Kumar & Kumari). According to history, from 8th century, the worship of virgin girls was a trend in Southern and Eastern India from Kanyakumari to Kamakshya. Later on it was added with Goddess of Lakshmi and the moon. Especially five days from Dussehra upto this full moon night, the young boys and girls celebrate this festival.

When the moon rises in the east horizon, people in villages get pleasure and play different games among themselves. This is also the birthday of 'Lord Kartikeya' the son of Lord Shiva. Worshipping Goddess Lakshmi is significance of this day. Girls take early bath in the morning and wear new clothes. They worship the Sun-God seven times by folded palm near their house deity Tulsi, the holy basil plant. At the evening, the girls prepare "Prasad" by crushing ripe banana, parched paddy (Kheel), cheese and make it in the form of moon. This is offered with utmost regard and respect to the Moon and the "Prasad" is distributed to others.

In all houses, worshipping of Goddess Lakshmi is performed. Fruits, Chida (boiled rice product), Coconut are offered to the Goddess. In rural areas there is a tradition of remaining wakeful throughout the night by playing different games, music etc. The girls in groups sing with rhythm the specific songs composed for full moon night, 'Kumar Purnima'. On this occasion the famous 'Puchi Dance' is played by them. This is a skilful exercise by sitting in squatting pose and rotating simultaneously by competition. The youngsters also play cards, shell-games, lido and dice etc and remain sleepless whole night. The boys covering up their bodies with branches and leaves of green trees act as ghosts and come nearer to other youngsters who have to recognize them without opening the dress of leaves. Similarly, some boys covering up their bodies with straw also pose as ghosts and come nearer to others to be recognized without opening the cover of straw.

It is believed that Goddess Lakshmi visits every house at this night and she offers her blessings of wealth to him who does not sleep tonight. Special Cakes (Gaintha), sweets and delicious foods are prepared in each house. Now days, grand worship of goddess Lakshmi is taking place in communities of towns and villages. In some famous towns, worship of Goddess Lakshmi called as 'Gaja Lakshmi Puja' is celebrated with music, orchestra and concerts. Large crowd assemble there to see the magnificent decoration of huge pandals, entrance gates, lightings, attractive statues of 'Gaja Lakshmi'.

FESTIVAL OF LIGHTS

(Diwali)

Diwali is celebrated on new moon day of month of Kartik **(Oct/ Nov)**. Everybody decorates his house by lighting lamps, candles, illuminating various types of coloured electric lights. Every house is cleaned and painted before Diwali. They enjoy the festival by wearing new dresses, distributing sweets and preparing delicious dishes. Some people observe fasting and worship goddess Lakshmi. Sweets are offered to the Goddess as Prasad. The Prasad is distributed among all after performing the puja. People purchase variety of crackers from many shops selling crackers in the main market and in streets. They fire those at their house premises at the night. Evening of Diwali is enjoyable with variety of lights and burning of crackers producing huge sound everywhere.

People offer obsequies (Shraadh) to their ancestors. In Odisha, the traders used to travel in the sea for trading in different countries in south East Asia. They return home before Dussehra and perform puja on Dussehra and Kumar Purnima. They offer obsequies (Shraddh) to their ancestors on Diwali and seek their blessings. After the 'Shraddh', they pray the ancestors who, by popular belief had arrived their house in darkness of Mahalaya-New-Moon(Mid September) and request them to bless the family members before leaving the house today in the festival of lights of auspicious Diwali (Mid October).

At the dead night worshipping of goddess 'Kali' takes place in communities. The worship of goddess is done through 'Tantrik Rites'.

As per the legend Lord Ramchandra after 14 yrs exile had entered Ayodhya on this day. On his arrival people of Ayodhya welcomed him celebrating grand festival by lighting earthen lamps and decorating the city.

On this day Lord Krishna had rescued the ladies (Gopies) of 'Gopapur' by killing the demon 'Tadkasur'. The ladies celebrate this day as the day of victory by lighting the entire city with earthen lamps. It is said that from that time the festival of Diwali is continuing.

It is also believed that Lord Krishna had sheltered and protected people of Gopapur from the anger of God 'Indra' by lifting the Gobardhan hill on this day. People celebrate this occasion by lighting lamps in their houses.

The 24th 'Tirthankar' of Jainism had expired on this day. Therefore, the Jain devotees celebrate this day by lighting lamps.

On this sacred day of Diwali the famous Shankaracharya had entered in the dead body and took rebirth. His devotees had celebrated this day by dancing, lighting lamps and igniting crackers.

Mughal emperor 'Akbar' used to celebrate the festival of Diwali. King Vikramaditya was crowned on the throne on this day. King Harshavardhan was also celebrating Diwali.

The festival of Diwali has not been limited to any religion and it has become a popular people's auspicious festival, in India. It is a public holiday in India and most of the working people visit their home on this holiday to celebrate this. On this occasion, people visit their relatives and friend's house for few days to greet and wish each other.

KARVA CHAUTH

'Karva Chauth' festival is celebrated in north and north-western part of India covering the states of Uttarakhand, UP, HP, J&K, Haryana, Punjab, Rajasthan and Gujrat. It falls on the fourth day of waning phase of moon or the dark fortnight (Krishna Paksha) of the Karthik month by the Hindu calendar following Autumnal Equinox **(October / November)**. A fast is kept by the married women to secure the long life of her husband.

THE RITUALS:

'Karva chauth' is considered one of the most important fasts observed by the married Hindu women. On this day the women pray for the welfare and long life of their husbands. Women begin preparation a few days in advance by buying cosmetics (shringar), traditional adornments or jewellery, and puja items, such as the Karva-lamps, matthi (a type of namkeen), henna and the decorated 'puja thali' (plate). The fast begins with dawn. They prepare food and have it before sunrise. The morning passes by festive activities like decorating hand and feet with heena, decorating the pooja-thali and meeting friends and relatives.

Fasting women do not eat during the day, and some additionally do not drink any water either. In traditional observance of the fast, the fasting woman does no house work. Women apply henna and other cosmetics to themselves and each other. The day passes in meeting friends and relatives. Parents often send gifts to their married daughters and their children.

In the late afternoon or evening, the ceremony by community women takes place. They gather at a common place like temple or a garden or someone's place who has arranged the Puja. They dress in fine clothing and wear jewellery and henna and dress in the complete finery of their wedding dresses. The dresses (sarees, lehenga, chunries, and salwars) are frequently red, gold, orange, pink in colour, which are considered auspicious colours. They adorn themselves with all other symbols of married women like nose pin, tika, bindi, chonp, bangles, earrings etc.

An elderly lady or the priest narrates the legend of 'Karva Chauth'. The essentials of this gathering is to listen the Karva Chauth story and establish a special mud pot, that is considered a symbol of lord Ganesha, a metal urn filled with water, flowers, idols of Ambika Gaur Mata, Goddess Parvati. In earlier times, an idol of Gaur Mata was made using earth and cow dung, which has now been replaced with an idol of Goddess Parvati. Women sit in a circle with their 'puja-thalis'. The song of Karva Chauth is collectively sung by the women as they perform the 'Feri' (passing their 'thali' around in the circle). They offer fruits, mathi, halwa, puri, sweets and food grains to the idols / deities. They then hand over these to their mother-in-law or sister-in-law.

After concluding the 'Fera' ceremony, the women await the rising of the moon. Once the moon is visible, it is customary for a fasting woman, with her husband nearby; to view its reflection in a vessel filled with water, through a sieve, or through the cloth of a 'dupatta'. Water is offered to the moon to secure its blessings. She then turns to her husband and views his face indirectly in the same manner. It is believed that the fasting women being spiritually strengthened can successfully confront and defeat death. The women pray, "Like the gold, the pearl and the moon may my suhaag (husband) always shine brightly". A husband now takes the water from the 'thali' and gives his wife her first sip and feeds her with the morsel of the day (usually sweet). The fast is now broken, and the woman has a complete meal.

It is customary for the husband to offer a gift to his wife, such as jewellery or a new dress. It is considered to be a romantic festival symbolizing the love between husband and wife. The festival thus empowers women as it enables them to quit housework completely for the day and expect gifts from their husbands. In the present day, groups of unmarried women also keep the fast together out of a sense of friendship. They observe the fast for their fiancés or for their desired husband.

SACROSANCT MOON

(Kartik Purnima)

Full moon day of month of Kartik is called 'Kartik Poornima' or 'Raas Poornima'. It occurs in the month of **November** every year. Hindus observe the month of Kartik as a very sacred and religious month. A number of festivals are therefore celebrated during this month. Those who observe their vow for the whole month, they take early morning bath then visit temple, pray their Gods and Goddess. Join mass eulogy, read epics and religious books (Bhagwat) and serve to the poor. They take holy food cooked with pure ghee and avoid rich oily, spicy dishes. Hindu widows celebrate this month up to full moon day with lot of devotion and sanctity. Everyday people worship their Gods in the temple and every evening they light earthen-lamps offering before their house Goddess 'Tulsi' (Holy Basil Plant).

Five days from the bright 21st day (Ekadashi) up to the full moon day are called as 'Bhishm Panchuk'. Those who cannot observe sacred vow for the whole month they can at least observe their vow for these five days. Nobody takes non-vegetarian food on these five days. It is believed that even the fish eating bird the crane, does not touch fish on these five days. Therefore, these five days are called as "Crane's Five Days Fasting".

Dance of Divine Love (Raas Leela): On the full moon day the famous aesthetic dance or act / play is celebrated which is termed as 'Raas Leela' i.e. "Dance of Divine Love". This dance is performed by boys and girls as a popular folk theatre. It depicts the story of love between Lord Krishna and his divine beloved 'Radha' performing aesthetic dance along with Gopis. Raas Leela has been a popular theme in Bharatnatyam, Odissy, Manipuri, Kuchipudi and Kathak dance forms. It symbolises romantic love between human beings in the material world as a reflection of the soul's original, ecstatic spiritual love for Lord Krishna in the spiritual world.

The traditional 'Raas Leela' performances in Vrindavan and Mathura are famous. The music remains the typical Dhrupada style with musical instruments like Sitar and Pakhawaj and the songs are sung in Vraja language, apparent to modern Hindi. At Shri Jagannath temple, Puri and at all the Iskon temples 'Raas Leela' is celebrated on this day and sacred vow is observed throughout the month. This is a prominent festival of devotees of Vaishnab cult. They worship the "Kalpataru" the famous banyan tree on this 'Kartik Poornima day'. To commemorate Raas Leela they worship 'Radha-Krishna' at the base of the banyan tree and offer the tree to Radha-Krishna.

This Karthik Purnima day is celebrated as the birthday of famous Sikh preceptor 'Guru Nanak. The Lord Kartikeya the elder son of Shiv Parvati also was born on this day therefore the Lord Kartikeya is worshiped this day.

Adoration of Boats (Boita Bandana): In the state of Odisha, this day is celebrated with 'Raas Leela' and observance of religious vow with worship for the whole month. This has another significant celebration in the state which commemorates Odisha's ancient maritime legacy. This day is considered the most auspicious day as in ancient days, the forefathers of Odisha were the traders who used to venture in their huge boats (Boitas) on journeys to distant lands like Bali, Java, Sumatra, Borneo and Ceylone (Sri Lanka). The great festival named as 'Bali Yatra', a hugely popular fair is held on the banks of river Mahanadi in the fort area of city of Cuttack. To celebrate the glory of ancient times the people in the state assemble at the bank of their nearest water bodies like river, pond, lake, canal etc and float small boats made of cork, coloured paper or banana trees barks lit by lamps placed within its hollow along with beetle leaf and beetle nuts.

This is called 'Adoration of Boats' (Boita Bandana). In the port town of Paradeep, Chandbali, Chandipur and Gopalpur this Bali Yatra is also observed.

Thus the Kartik Poornima is an all India festival on view point of social, cultural, historical and religious feelings.

Prathma Ashtami

The 8th day of dark fortnight of month of 'Margashir' is called 'Prathma Ashtami' which normally falls in the middle of **November**. This is a traditional people's family festival. It is also celebrated in the famous Lingraaj temple at Bhubaneswar. The Lord Lingraaj travels to his maternal uncle's house by wearing new clothes.

'Prathma Ashtami' is a rite held for the life and prosperity of eldest child who is offered a lighted lamp ovation by the mother and senior female relatives followed by elaborate rituals. The child is smeared with vermillion, sandal paste, flowers and he / she is adorned with doob-grass and sacred rice-grains. It is customary that the maternal uncle provides new clothes to the child. Five grains, five leaves, five flowers are offered to the Gods including Lord Ganesh and are invited to the water filled pitcher covered with coconut and mango leaves which is worshipped with offering of five types of sweetmeats, cakes, curies, etc as food-offering by the family. New clothes of the child are worshipped with the sacred pitcher. The child is given to wear these new clothes after the worship.

Enduri: A specific cake in Odisha is prepared on this day named as 'Enduri'. This cake is prepared by placing the mixed paste of daal and rice inside the turmeric leaf. It is then kept over a water filled earthen pot which is heated on an oven. The cake is thus boiled and prepared by the steam of the water and is very delicious and hygienic. Thus the main delicacy of the day is the cake 'Enduri'.

It is learnt that from 14th century onwards 'Prathma Ashtami' was given recognition as people's festival in Odisha. This is also called as 'Fateful-Ashtami' (Soubhagini Ashtami). By the occasion of Ashtami, yield of good crops are noticed. Due to the good harvest, the farmers get pleased and feel themselves fortunate by this time.

According to the great epic 'Skandh Puraan', the God 'Kaal Bhairav' is worshipped on this day. Therefore, Prathma Ashtami is also called 'Kaal Bhairava Ashtami'. In some of our epics it has been also named as 'Paap-Nashini Ashtami' (Sin-Dispelling Day).

CHHAT PUJA

In eastern India, especially in the state of Bihar, 'Chhat Puja' is an important festival. This festival occurs twice in a year during month of Baisakh **(May)**and Kartik **(November)**. The community festival is celebrated in honour of the Sun God and celebrations go on for 4 days. In month of November it falls on 6th day after Diwali and is the main celebration of 'Chhat'.

Amongst the women folk, there is a lot of excitement and preparations start weeks in advance. Temporary shrines are made from stalks of sugarcane and the entire family together sing hymns in praise of Sun-God. Each shrine contains terracotta elephants, several small lamps and offerings of rice and fruits are made around it. Women make food for the Sun-God and men sit out side the house on guard. Later they guard the baskets of "Prasad" at the riverside.

Chhat is a way to be grateful to the Sun for giving the bounties of life on earth and for the fulfilment of wishes of believers. It is a festival of reverence to the solar deity with prayer and appeasement observed with soberness. It is the festival of truth, non-violence, forgiveness, compassion and is held in high esteem and regard. The setting Sun as well as the rising Sun are celebrated during Chhat for Sun-God's glory as the cycle of birth starts with death. The Sun considered the God of energy and of the life force is worshipped to promote well being, prosperity and progress. The ritual of the festival is vigorous including holy bathing, fasting, abstaining from drinking water, standing in water for long periods of time, offering prayer, lighted lamp and "Prasad" to setting and rising Sun. It follows a period of abstinence, segregation of the worshiper observing ritual purity and sleeping on the floor on a single blanket. The festival does not involve any priest or pandit.

Chhat Ghat: The womenfolk carry baskets containing food, flowers, sandal wood, vermillion, rice and fruits usually covered with saffron coloured cotton cloth an offering to Sun-God to the nearest river or lake. Then they stand half dipped inside the water for many hours chanting hymns and paying obeisance to Sun-God at Sun set and Sun rise. Be it a cold day or hot, they keep on standing in water offering handful of water to the rising Sun. Some undertake even harder vows if their wishes are fulfilled. After immersion and offerings, the food is considered blessed and then the women, who had been fasting for almost two days, break their fast with this "Prasad" of Sun-God. The devotees along with family and friends go to the river bank. The occasion is almost a carnival. The Chhat has so much importance that even millionaire beg for "Prasad" at the Chhat Ghat. This symbolizes that all persons are beggar in front of the almighty. According to belief if you beg for the "Prasad" all wishes will come true.

Fairs are organized along the river front, with different stalls of food and entertainment. 'Chhat' festival is an important event and is observed with dedication and devotion. It fosters the spirit of community worship, sharing, faith and perseverance.

MUHARRAM

Muharram festival commemorates the martyrdom of **Hazrat Imam Hussain**, the grandson of the Holy Prophet. This festival starts at the 1ˢᵗ day of Muharram and lasts for 10 days. Muharram is the first month of Islamic calendar and generally falls in November to December.

After the demise of the Chief Muslim ruler, Hazrat Ali, dispute and disagreement resulted among Muslims on the question of succession. During this month, while on a journey, Hazrat Hussain, his family members and a number of his followers were surrounded by the forces of Yazid, the Muslim ruler of that time. During the siege, they were deprived of food and water and many of them were put to death. The incident happened at a place called **Karbala** in Iraq. His violent death to this day awakens the sympathy of the faithful who commemorate his martyrdom with sorrow and indignation.

Some sects of Muslims hold meeting delivering speeches on the happenings of Karbala and on the lives of martyrs. Some put on black clothes symbolising mourning. Assemblies **(Majalis)** are held every day during the first nine days where orators relate the incident of the martyrdom of Hazrat Hussain in a great detail. On the 10ᵗʰ day of Muharram, large processions are formed and the devoted followers parade the streets holding banners and carrying models of a mausoleum of Hazrat and his people, who fell at Karbala. They show their grief and sorrow by inflicting wounds on their own bodies with sharp metal tied to chain with which they scourge themselves. This is done in order to depict the sufferings of the martyrs. It is a sad occasion and everyone in the procession chants **"Ya Hussain"**, with loud wails of lamentation.

Generally a white horse beautifully decorated for the occasion, is also included in the procession, to mark the empty mount of Hazrat Hussain after his martyrdom. During these first ten days of Muharram, drinking posts are also set up temporarily where water and juices are served to all, free of charge.

After appearance of new moon, people assemble in the **Imambara** (lit, enclosure of Imam), a permanent meeting place built in stone. There they recite the Fatihah over some sherbet (sweetened, cool drink), rice or sugar in Husain's name. The cool drink is meant to remind the faithful of the terrible thirst Hussain and his family and retinue had to suffer. Food and drink are later distributed to the public, especially to the poor. In some places a pit is dug in which a fire is lighted every evening of the festival, and young and old people fence across it with sticks of sword or they run around it calling out: **Ya Hussain!**

The Imambara, too, is decorated. Inside are placed the tazias or tabuts, wooden structures covered with silver paper, coloured paper and tinsel fringes. They are made with imagination and artistic sense and are meant to represent Husain's mausoleum, erected on the plains of Karbala, or else the Prophet's tomb at Medina or even the Taj Mahal of Agra. Every evening people hold gatherings and perform elaborate artistic traditions, they narrate the heartless way in which Yazid's men killed Husain and his family and retinue. Repeatedly the assembled faithful mob rise from their places and with grief beat their chests (sinah-bazi) crying out: 'Ya Husain' and cursing Yazid, the caliph responsible for Husain's death. Men and boys, naked from the waist, beat themselves with a bundle of sharp blades so that the blood streams down their backs or, forming a large group, they beat their chests in a uniform rhythm crying together.

On the evening of the twelfth day people sit up all night, reading the Quran and reciting marsiyahs and verses in honour of Husain. On the thirteenth day a quantity of food is cooked and, after saying the fatihah over it, it is given to the poor. With this act of charity the Muharram celebrations end.

GLORY OF GODDESS MAHALAKSHMI

In the month of 'Margasir' **(Nov-Dec)**, on every Thursday Goddess Mahalakshmi is worshipped with utmost devotion by women. Thursday is the auspicious day for worshipping Mahalakshmi who as per Hindu belief is the embodiment of all wealth and food materials. Paddy is the staple grain and cultivation of paddy is the prime agriculture in the state. This is the harvest season for paddy. Women of every house get fully involved in worshipping the Goddess.

'Chitaa' (Jhoti): They clean the house thoroughly on the previous day i.e. Wednesday. In villages people after cleaning their houses besmear their court yard and their mud walls with cow dung water which is taken as sacred. It is believed that Goddess Lakshmi would never visit the house if the house is dirty and untidy. The entrance as well as the doorstep of the house is decorated by women with artistic drawings by using rice-paste resembling like white coloured paints. They take the rice paste in a bowl and draw arts on the floor by dint of their fingers soaked in the rice paste. They make footprints of Goddess Mahalakshmi along with attractive flowers and leaves, thereby inviting the Goddess to the house. The outer walls of the house and the galleries are also decorated by drawing such arts. This is called 'Chita' (Jhoti) by which they welcome goddess Mahalakshmi to enter their house through the steps of their entrance door.

Mana: They wake up very early in the morning at 04:00 Hrs on Thursday, take bath and prepare for 'Lakshmi Pooja'. They light an earthen-lamp of ghee and place it at the entrance door. In rural areas and villages, a pot made of bamboo-canes measuring the paddy known as 'Mana' is filled up to the brink with freshly harvest paddy. Rice and lentils are also kept with the paddy. The 'Mana' is the symbol of Mahalakshmi.

Others worship Lakshmi by placing her idol or photo frame on the stool in the house. Adoration of the Goddess is done by offering fruits, coconut, banana, doob-grass, amla, curd, turmeric, flowers, incense etc. It is customary to read out the holy book, the Eulogy, 'Lakshmi Puran' while performing pooja. This eulogy was written by the ancient poet 'Balram Das' and is read by the house lady while performing the worship and others listen with devotion. It is believed that the Goddess Lakshmi visits every house during pooja.

Lakshmi Puran depicts the story of Lord Jagannath and his elder brother Lord Balbhadra who had suffered a lot in the absence of Lakshmi. One day Lakshmi had visited the house of her devotee, a lady from very backward and lower class. Balbhadra objected to this and persuaded Jagannath to drive out Lakshmi from the temple. Lakshmi left the temple and was angry with these two brothers. Due to her agony, the brothers became poor, did not get food, wandered as two poor Brahmins begging on the streets. Ultimately, they arrived at the palace of Lakshmi situated in the area of lower class and asked for food. Lakshmi served them food and the brothers took it with satisfaction. They could recognize Lakshmi by the taste of the preparation of food. They repented for their mistake and requested Lakshmi to come back to the temple. Lakshmi made the condition that she will go back to the temple if the feeling of upper and lower class, rich and poor, Brahmin and backward, untouchability etc will be dispelled from the temple (Sri Mandir). After getting the commitment from Lord Jagannath Mahalakshmi went back to the temple.

All the places in India observe this festival from very ancient time. This festival is not only performed by Hindus but also being celebrated by the 'Ghesi' cult of Islam religion. Lakshmi pooja is also celebrated in Indo-China.

Manabasa: The importance of this worship known as 'Manabasa' is (i) Spiritual—by adoration of the Goddess Mahalakshmi (ii)

Agricultural—by worshipping paddy, rice and pulses (iii) Social—ladies are the symbol of power and are never to be ignored. Even God had surrendered before the power of woman (IV) Moral—there should not be any feeling for upper and lower class and un-touchability in the society.

BLOOMING NEW MOON

(Bakul Amabasya)

On the new-moon day of month of **December** (Pausha), this festival is celebrated in village-houses. Mango is the king of fruits and mango trees, these days bloom with buds to bear mango fruits in the ensuing spring season. All our villages are full of mango trees and their branches blossom laden with flowers to produce mango buds. In religious feelings, mango tree has lots of priority. Its leaves, branches, flowers, buds, woods and the fruits, all these are utilized as worshipping material before the God. In the temples, in festivals and in religious observances; the branches of mango tree generate holiness, purity and sanctity.

Gaintha Cake: On this day, no particular God or Goddess is worshipped. Only the sacred mango tree is worshipped with offering of special cakes. Family members gather near their own mango tree and perform the worship of the tree. A special cake called 'Gaintha' is prepared by ladies of every house with a unique technique. The raw rice is crushed to powder and then this powder soaked with water is boiled. The boiled crushed rice is manually shaped in the form of a cake of various sizes up to maximum 2 inch x 5 inch. Some cakes are filled inside with sweet cheese, molasses / sugar and spices. An earthen pot or a vessel is half filled with water. A cage type base or stage is framed out of thin bamboo-sticks inside the empty space of the vessel above the water. The handmade 'Gaintha' cakes are placed on the frame on this bamboo frame and the vessel is heated over an oven and the face of the vessel is covered by a lid. The cakes are thus heated by steam inside the vessel for some time and get prepared. Every house celebrates this festival by preparing 'Gaintha' and a variety of other cakes.

In the famous Jagannath temple the mango flower buds with 'Gaintha' called as 'Baula Gaintha' is offered to the Trinity-Lords, while worshipping them on this auspicious day. A special worship with decoration of the Lords takes place. It is believed that whoever witnesses this mango-bud adoration / invocation of the Deities at Jagannath temple, Puri he deserves to proceed to the heaven.

There is another great importance of this day. The Lord-God of Hindus in His 3rd incarnation took birth in the form of a 'Boar' (Barah Avtaar) on this sacred day.

CHRISTMAS

The festival of Christmas celebrates the birth of **Jesus Christ on 25ᵗʰ December** and conveys his message of love, tolerance and brotherhood. Jesus was born in a stable in the town of Bethlehem, to the Virgin Mary, supported by Joseph (her husband). It is believed that angels heralded the child's arrival and told the shepherds about it. Three wise kings were also told about Jesus' birth. A star guided the shepherds and the three wise kings to the stable, where they offered obeisance and gave gifts to the infant who was God's son on earth. Gifts and presents thus form an integral part of the festival during Christmas. It is believed that Saint Nicolas in the guise of the exuberant Santa Claus comes riding a reindeer-drawn sleigh at night and distributes gifts to the children.

It is the most important festival of Indian Christians. They have adopted this Christian festival as a part of Indian culture and many of the rituals have been modified to suite the climatic conditions of the land. They decorate banana or mango trees instead of traditional pine trees. They light up small oil-burning lamps as Christmas decorations and feel their churches with red flowers. As a part of their celebration they give Christmas gifts to their family members and token of money to poor people as charity. People decorate their houses and churches with flowers for the midnight mass. They put small clay lamps on the rooftops and walls of their houses at Christmas, just as the Hindus do during their festival called Diwali. They decorate their houses with mango leaves. Churches often have an Evening Service on Christmas and are fabulously decorated with poinsettia flowers and candles. Carolling processions on streets and thorough fares are also seen.

Famous Christmas themes contain the promotion of peace, goodwill and compassion. Customs contain the show of **Holy Christmas trees** and Nativity scenes, the exchange of cards and gifts and the coming of Santa Claus (Father Christmas) on Christmas morning or Christmas Eve. **Nativity Scenes** traditionally contain the Three Wise Men who were first told about birth of Jesus namely Caspar, Balthazar and Melchior. Famous holiday trees are decorated with poinsettia, red amaryllis, holy Christmas cactus and mistletoe.

In different businesses, communities, schools and nations have Christmas dances and parties in the weeks before this festival. Christmas shows can contain a retelling of the tale of Christ's birth. Groupings might stay neighbourhood homes for singing carols. Other holds fundraising drives or do volunteer job for help. Since there are only six more days left for the New Year, people wish each other '**Merry Christmas and Happy New Year**'. Fun, frolic, and laughter mark this year-end festival. Jubilation, parties and gaiety continue till the New Year.

On Christmas Eve or Christmas Day, a particular meal is generally offered. In several areas, treats and candy are also part of Christmas celebration.